AF445452

THE GOLDEN GAP

THE LIFE STRATEGY SERIES

—

BOOK ONE

The Leverage Code
Build position before you need it

BOOK TWO

Spat-Out
Survive the hit when it comes

BOOK THREE

The Golden Gap
Reclaim, Reset, and Reposition Your Life After 50

THE GOLDEN GAP

Reclaim, Reset, and Reposition Your Life After 50

MJ Carver

MJ Squared Group

Copyright © 2025 MJ Carver

All rights reserved.

No part of this publication may be reproduced, distributed, or transmitted in any form or by any means, including photocopying, recording, or other electronic or mechanical methods, without the prior written permission of the publisher, except in the case of brief quotations embodied in critical reviews and certain other noncommercial uses permitted by copyright law.

The information in this book is provided for educational and informational purposes only. It does not constitute financial, legal, medical, or investment advice. The author and publisher are not responsible for any actions taken based on the contents of this book. Readers should consult qualified professionals for advice specific to their individual circumstances.

Names, characters, places, and real-world locations mentioned are used for illustrative purposes. Cost-of-living figures, financial data, and travel costs reflect documented real-world research as of the time of writing and are subject to change.

ISBN (eBook / Audiobook): 979-8-9954245-5-0

ISBN (Paperback): 979-8-9954245-4-3

Published by MJ Squared Group
First Edition, 2025
Printed in the United States of America

DEDICATION

For anyone ready to reclaim their life — at any point in their life.

For those who have learned how valuable their life and career experience truly is,

who are brave enough to combine it all,

and who are ready to stop and truly listen

to the unusual birds in a foreign country —

or somewhere they have always wanted to go.

Contents

Introduction..*i*

THE CASE

Chapter One
The 35-Year Sentence....................17

Chapter Two
The Retirement Trap....................31

Chapter Three
The Movement Nobody Named..........61

Chapter Four
Who Takes the Golden Gap...............77

Chapter Five
What a Gap Actually Is......................93

THE NUMBERS

Chapter Six
The Cash Snapshot: Living Lean and Eating Well....................111

Chapter Seven
The Numbers....................127

THE LIVED EXPERIENCE

Chapter Eight
The Four Stages of the Gap...............151

Chapter Nine
Who Are You Without the Title?.......171

Chapter Ten
The Relationship Reset....................191

Chapter Eleven
The Family Equation....................205

Chapter Twelve
The External Skeptics and the Internal Skeptic..................................219

Chapter Thirteen
The Gap Is a Living Laboratory.......233

THE PRACTICE

Chapter Fourteen
Slow Travel: The Philosophy and the Practice................................251

Chapter Fifteen
The Entry Point...................279

Chapter Sixteen
The Weekly Architecture.................295

THE PREPARATION

Chapter Seventeen
The Pre-Gap Timeline: 12 Months Out
....309

Chapter Eighteen
The Pre-Gap Timeline: 6 Months Out
....325

Chapter Nineteen

The Pre-Gap Timeline: Final 90 Days
....339

WHAT COMES AFTER

Chapter Twenty
The Gap Doesn't End.........................353

A Closing Letter to the Reader.............365
A Note on Research............................371
About the Author...............................374
Also by MJ Carver.............................374

The Choice You Keep Making

You made the choice.

You did not make it carelessly. You made it the way you made all the important choices during the career years — deliberately, responsibly, with the full weight of your professional judgment behind it. The new project needed someone with your experience. The timing was difficult. There would be other chances.

You told your friends you would visit them next time. You told your partner you would see the Northern Lights someday. You told yourself that the right choice for your career was the right choice for your life, and you believed it, and you were not entirely wrong.

But here you are.

And the friends are still on the other side of the country. And the Northern Lights are still up there, arcing across the sky above Iceland and Norway and Lapland on winter nights while you sleep in the same bed in the same house in the same city where you have slept for twenty years. And the project you chose instead — the project that needed you, that only you could lead, that justified the decision — you can barely remember what it was about.

This is not a book about regret. But it begins here, because regret is honest in a way that aspiration is not.

Regret does not ask whether you had good reasons. It does not care about the quarterly numbers or the promotion or the performance review that reflected your dedication. Regret asks a simpler question. Did you do the things that mattered to you, while you still could?

For most people reading this book, the honest answer is: not enough.

Not enough trips. Not enough mornings in places that were not home. Not enough dinners where you and your partner had something genuinely new to tell each other — something that happened apart, something that required the other person to lean in and ask what happened next. Not enough time in foreign cities where nobody knew your title and the day was entirely yours. Not enough standing in front of things that were extraordinary and letting them be extraordinary instead of photographing them and moving to the next one.

You watched other people go. You saw their photographs and felt something you may not have named but recognized — a specific, low-level ache that is not quite envy and not quite sadness and is, if you are honest, regret. Not for their trip. For the version of your own life in which you made the different choice.

—

Here is what I know about the person reading this book.

You are not someone who wasted your years. You built something. You showed up. You provided, contributed, advanced, accumulated. The career gave real things to real people — your family, your colleagues, the organization you served. The choices you made were not foolish. They were the choices of someone who took their responsibilities seriously.

But responsibilities have a way of expanding to fill every available space. The career that was supposed to serve your life gradually became your life. The two days you were promised as the reward for the five became the brief recovery from the five rather than the life you were actually living. And somewhere in the accumulated weight of all those responsible choices, the things that were specifically, personally, irreplaceably yours got deferred.

The friends you were going to visit. The pilgrimage you were going to walk. The continent you were going to spend three months inhabiting rather than two weeks visiting. The version of your marriage that had something new to discuss at dinner because you had both been somewhere the other had not been and come back with a story worth telling.

Deferred. Not cancelled. Deferred.

The difference between deferred and cancelled is a window. And the window, if you are reading this book, is still open.

Barely. But open.

The Stairs

There is a specific image I want you to sit with.

The stairs to the Sydney Opera House.

Not the building itself — the stairs. The long sweep of stone steps that rise from the harbor forecourt to the entrance, the ones you have seen in a thousand photographs, the ones that every visitor climbs with the harbor bridge behind them and the water catching the light below.

You can climb those stairs right now. Your body will carry you up them without drama, without special preparation, without the careful negotiation with your knees that will one day be required. You can climb them and stand at the top and turn around and look at what is behind you and feel what that feels like.

There is a version of you in the future who cannot do this. Not because something terrible happened — because time happened. The gradual renegotiation that age conducts quietly, without announcement, until one day the terms have changed enough that the stairs are a different proposition than they once were.

That future version of you will know that you could have climbed those stairs. Will know that the window was open and the body was capable and the resources were sufficient and the only thing that stood between you and the top of those stairs was the choice you made.

Which choice do you want that future version of you to be remembering?

The Northern Lights do not care whether your project succeeded. The Camino de Santiago does not know your title. The dinner table where you and your partner finally had something genuinely new to talk about does not require your performance review to have been outstanding.

They require only that you showed up while showing up was fully possible.

The Honest Numbers

Will this hurt your savings?

It sure will. Let me be direct about that because this book will not be honest if it pretends otherwise.

The Golden Gap — the deliberately designed period of reset, exploration, and reinvention that this book proposes — costs money. Not as much as you think. Not nearly as much as the suburban American life that the Convenience Premium has quietly inflated over decades of trading money for the time you did not have. Two people living the slow travel life that this book describes have documented spending an average of $28,050 per year across four continents and nineteen countries. That is less than most American couples spend on housing alone.

But it is not free. And the years of the Golden Gap are years in which your portfolio is being drawn down rather than built up, in which earned income has paused or slowed, in which the financial accumulation that defined the career phase is not happening in the same way.

That is a real cost. Anyone who tells you otherwise is not being straight with you.

Here is what regret costs.

Regret does not appear on a balance sheet. It does not have a line item. It does not compound at 7% per year or get reported in a quarterly statement. It accumulates in a different register entirely — in the quiet moments when you see a photograph of somewhere you have never been, in the dinner conversation that circles the same territory it has circled for years, in the body that is slightly less capable than it was last year and slightly more capable than it will be next year, in the knowledge that the window you believed was permanent has been getting smaller the whole time.

You can measure the financial cost of the Golden Gap precisely. You can calculate the portfolio drawdown, the foregone compounding, the reduced balance at sixty-five or seventy. The number is real and a good financial advisor will help you understand it exactly.

You cannot measure the cost of the Northern Lights you did not see. You cannot calculate the value of the morning you and your partner stood at the top of a hill in Portugal with nowhere to be and nothing required of you and looked at each other with genuine curiosity rather than the comfortable familiarity that long marriages sometimes mistake for intimacy. You cannot quantify what it would have meant to walk the Camino de Santiago while your knees still allowed it, or to spend three months in Southeast Asia while the body can handle the heat and the pace, or to have something to tell your

grandchildren that is actually worth
telling.

Both costs are real. Only one of them can
be planned for. The other one simply
accumulates.

The question this book is asking is not
whether you can afford the Golden Gap.

The question is whether you can afford to
keep making the same choice.

What This Book Is

This is not a travel guide. There are
excellent travel guides. This is not one of
them.

This is not a retirement planning manual.
The financial dimension of the Golden Gap
is real and this book addresses it honestly,
with specific numbers and actionable
strategies. But the money is not the point.
The money is what makes the point
possible.

This is not a bucket list toolkit. The bucket
list mentality is actually a version of the
same problem — the accumulation of
experiences as things to be checked off
rather than lived. The Golden Gap is not a
list. It is a life.

This is a design document for the most important window of your adult life.

The Golden Gap is the deliberately designed period of reset, exploration, and reinvention taken at the specific moment when health, wealth, and time align — before age quietly renegotiates the terms of what is possible. That window falls, for most people, between the ages of fifty and sixty-five. It may be open right now. It is almost certainly narrowing.

This book is the comprehensive guide to using it.

The first section makes the case. The retirement model that was sold to you is broken. The financial math of the Golden Gap is better than you think. The version of you that can do this fully is available right now and will not always be.

The middle section covers the lived experience — the psychological journey of who you are when the title is gone, the identity transition, the relationship reset, the family equation, the skeptics you will encounter both outside and inside your own head. It is also where the laboratory opens: the gap as an active experiment in which you test assumptions about yourself that the career never had time or space to run.

The practical section covers the how. Slow travel as a philosophy and a financial strategy. The base camp model and where to go first. The weekly architecture that gives the gap enough structure without recreating the schedule you left. What comes after — the three paths forward and the insight that the gap, once taken, does not have to end when you book the flight home.

The final section is the preparation — the comprehensive three-chapter pre-gap timeline that takes you from twelve months out to the day before departure, covering everything from the home decision to the insurance architecture to the medication strategy to what the first week will actually feel like.

And throughout, woven into every chapter, is the honest account of someone who made the choice — who took the Golden Gap, who is living it right now, in Sydney and beyond, stopping on the coastal path to watch waves crash into rocks because his wife reminded him the laptop would still be there in an hour.

There is always time.

That is the point.

The Choice

You made the choice to take the new project instead of visiting your friends.

You made the choice to defer the Northern Lights.

You made dozens of choices that felt like the right choices at the time — responsible, professional, serious choices that served the career and the family and the organization and the accumulation. And many of them were right. The career produced real things. The choices were not foolish.

But there were two kinds of choices in those years, and you made one kind much more often than the other. You chose the work over the experience. The project over the trip. The responsible deferral over the irreplaceable now.

You have just enough left. Enough health. Enough wealth. Enough time. Not infinite amounts of any of them — but enough, right now, in this specific configuration, to make the different choice.

The Northern Lights are still there.

The stairs to the Sydney Opera House are still climbable.

The Camino de Santiago has been walked by people your age for a thousand years, and it is waiting.

Your partner is sitting across from you at a dinner table where the conversation has been circling the same territory for longer than either of you would like to admit, and somewhere in that person is the version of them you fell in love with, who was curious and surprising and full of things you had not heard yet, and that version is recoverable — but it requires something new to happen.

This book is about making the different choice.

Not someday. Not when conditions are perfect. Not when the savings are at the number and the kids are fully launched and the timing finally aligns.

Now.

While the window is open.

Are you ready to choose your Golden Gap?

—

Five Things to Know Before You Read Further

One: This book is written for people over fifty who have built something and are wondering what comes next. If that is not you, the book may still be useful, but it was written for you.

Two: The specific framework, strategies, and financial data in this book reflect research, documented real-world experience, and ongoing personal practice. The numbers are real. The options are real. The choices are yours.

Three: This is Book Three of The Life Strategy Series. Book One — The Leverage Code — is about building position before you need it. Book Two — Spat-Out — is about surviving the hit when it comes. This book is about using the window before it closes.

Four: The Golden Gap looks different for everyone who takes it. This book recognizes six distinct types of gap-taker — from the person whose company made the decision for them to the person who has been planning this for years. You will meet all six in Chapter Four and recognize yourself in at least one. The framework is a starting point, not a prescription. Your gap will be yours — designed by you, for you, with the specific curiosity and capability and history that only you have.

Five: The regret you feel when you read the opening pages of this book is information. It is telling you something real about what you want and what you have been deferring. Do not dismiss it. Do not manage it. Read what it is saying.

Then make the different choice.

THE CASE

Chapters 1 – 5

The case for the Golden Gap

CHAPTER ONE

The 35-Year Sentence

Nobody warned you it would feel like this.

Not the bad parts — you knew there would be bad parts. Every career has them. The difficult manager, the unreasonable deadline, the reorg that scrambled everything you had built, the year when nothing went right and the metrics said so in language that left nowhere to hide. You knew those were coming. You signed up for them anyway.

What nobody warned you about was the accumulation.

The way a career does not arrive all at once but builds, year by year, in layers you barely notice as they settle. The way the structure that organized your days also quietly consumed them. The energy the job required went somewhere else — and what it went somewhere else from was the rest of your life — the friendships that thinned because you were always tired or always traveling, the hobbies that never quite materialized because there was never quite enough of you left over, the dinners that did not happen because the week had taken everything and the weekend was for recovery.

You did not notice this happening because you were inside it. That is the nature of accumulation. You only see it from outside.

The outside came later. Sometimes it came because the company ended the arrangement. Sometimes it came because you ended it yourself. Sometimes it comes because you are reading this book and something in the introduction named a feeling you have been carrying for years without quite having the words for it.

However you arrived at the outside, you are here now. And from here, you can see the shape of what the sentence actually was.

What the Career Actually Was

Let me tell you what I mean by sentence.

Not a punishment. A structure. The same word does both jobs and both meanings are accurate.

A career is a structure that organizes your life around external requirements. The job needs you at a certain place at a certain time doing a certain set of things to a certain standard. It measures you against metrics. It compensates you for compliance and performance. It provides identity, purpose, income, social connection, and a reason to get out of bed on Monday morning — and in exchange it takes your time, your energy, your headspace, and a significant portion of your best years.

This is not a criticism. The trade was real on both sides. The career gave genuine things. For most people reading this book, it gave enough to raise a family, build a home, accumulate something. It gave competence — the deep, hard-won, specific kind that only comes from sustained practice under real conditions. It gave relationships, even if those relationships thinned over time. It gave the satisfaction of problems solved, teams built, results delivered.

But the trade was still a trade. And trades have costs.

My industry was one that ran when other people rested. While the rest of the country took their weekends, took their holidays, gathered for their Sunday lunches and their Friday nights out, the work continued. The operation did not pause for the calendar. The customers did not stop needing things because it was a holiday. And so we showed up when they needed us, which was when everyone else was off, which meant that the rhythms that organize social life — the rhythms that produce friendships and dinner parties and the slow accumulated fabric of a community — never quite applied to us.

This is not uncommon in certain industries. But it is also not the norm. The wall street banker works brutal hours but works them on a schedule the rest of the world understands. The surgeon is on call but the on-call follows a rotation. My industry had its own logic, its own clock, its own relationship with time that was simply different from the one most people inhabit — and that difference, compounded over thirty-five years, adds up to a life that looks different from the outside than it felt from the inside.

From the inside, it felt like work. Like showing up, solving problems, managing people, delivering results. Like doing what needed to be done because someone had to do it and you were the one who did it.

From the outside, it looks like the thing that happened instead of the other things.

The Microscope

Here is something that changed during the career years that nobody fully anticipated when it started.

The measurement got more sophisticated.

In the early years, the metrics were blunt instruments. Numbers that told a rough story. Sales figures, operational data, customer feedback that arrived slowly and in aggregate. You knew when things were going well and when they were not. So did your manager. The conversation was imprecise but human.

Then the technology arrived.

Not all at once. Gradually, in waves, each one more comprehensive than the last. Enterprise software systems that tracked everything in real time. Dashboards that let someone in an air-conditioned corporate office see exactly what was happening at every location, at every hour, with every metric rendered in color-coded precision.

The old microscope looked at a slide of material and gave you a flat image. The new microscope builds a three-dimensional model of your performance and turns it over. Looks at it from the side. Looks at it from underneath. Sees inside it. The data that used to arrive weekly arrived daily. Then hourly. Then in real time, on screens in offices hundreds of miles away, reviewed by people who had never walked the floor you walked.

I walked ten to twenty miles a day as part of my job. In heat that could reach a hundred degrees. Moving weight that over a weekend added up to a ton or more. My body was doing this while the enterprise software was dissecting my output in three dimensions and the results were being reviewed in climates that bore no relationship to the climate I was working in.

This is not unique to my industry. The microscope got more powerful everywhere. The technology that was supposed to make work more efficient mostly made work more measurable, and more measurable mostly meant more accountable, and more accountable mostly meant more pressure.

The wall street banker worried about their numbers. The surgeon worried about their outcomes. You worried about yours. We all worried about results, in increasingly granular detail, with increasingly sophisticated tools that could identify, isolate, and examine every variable of our performance in ways that would have been impossible a decade earlier.

The career did not just take your time. In the later years, it took your sense of being observed. The specific, low-level stress of knowing that the work was being watched in real time, measured in real time, evaluated in real time — that stress does not announce itself. It settles. It becomes part of the background of professional life the way that traffic noise becomes part of the background of city life. You stop noticing it. But it is still there, still consuming something, still running in the background while you are trying to be present for everything else.

What the Days Off Actually Were

Here is the honest version of what recovery looked like.

The days off were not leisure. Not really. They were recovery from the days on. The body that had walked twenty miles needed to not walk twenty miles for a day. The mind that had been solving problems and managing people and watching metrics needed to not do those things for a day. The specific tiredness of sustained professional performance is not the kind of tiredness that a good night's sleep resolves. It is cumulative. It requires time. More time, as the years go on, than the days off can provide.

I had no hobbies. Not because I lacked curiosity — the curiosity was there, locked in the box that the career kept on the high shelf. But hobbies require something beyond the minimum — a surplus of energy and attention and time that can be directed toward something with no practical return. The career consumed the surplus. What remained went to the basics. Food, sleep, whatever maintenance the body and the household required. And then back to Monday.

I had no close friends in the conventional sense. The industry I worked in created acquaintances — the people you worked alongside at a location, the colleagues you collaborated with on a project, the contacts who knew your professional reputation and respected it. These are real relationships. They are not the same as friends. Friends require availability, the kind that comes from living on the same schedule as the rest of the world, being free for the spontaneous Saturday and the standing Friday dinner and the gradual accumulation of shared ordinary life that produces genuine intimacy.

I was not on the same schedule as the rest of the world. My schedule was its own thing, and it produced its own kind of connection — real, valuable, specific — but not the same as what the people who worked nine to five in the same city for thirty years had with the people they worked alongside.

There were good things. I want to be clear about this. The career was not only cost.

There were experiences that the career made possible — brief but genuine, the kind that stay with you. There were places seen and problems solved and people helped and results delivered that mattered. There was competence built at a level that only sustained practice under real conditions can produce. There was the specific satisfaction of having done something difficult and done it well, repeatedly, over a long time.

The trade was real on both sides.

But the trade was still a trade. And the brief, genuine experiences were brief. That is the thing. They were just enough to sustain the belief that this was a life fully lived. Just enough to make the next period of accumulation feel temporary. Just enough to defer the question of what a life that was not organized around the trade might actually look like.

The Moment You Saw the Structure

There is a specific moment — different for every person, but recognizable to almost all of them — when the career stops being the environment you inhabit and becomes the structure you can see from outside.

For some people it is sudden. The Spat-Out moment. The company making the decision before you did. The restructuring that removed the role you had spent years building. The involuntary exit that forced

the view from outside before you were
ready for it.

For others it arrives more gradually. A
Sunday evening with a particular quality of
dread — not about anything specific, just
about Monday. A moment of looking at a
colleague who retired and noticing
something in their face that you cannot
quite name. A vacation that showed you,
briefly, what it felt like to have your time
actually belong to you — and then ended
and sent you back.

For others it arrives through contrast. A
conversation with someone who seems
genuinely free in a way you cannot fully
articulate. A photograph of somewhere you
have never been that produces a feeling
you do not examine too closely. A dinner
table with nothing new on it.

However it arrives, the moment is the
same in its essential quality. You see the
structure. You see that the thing which
organized your life is a structure — not
permanent, not inevitable, not the only
possible way to spend the years that
remain. A structure you entered
deliberately, inhabited fully, and can now
choose to exit.

This is the threshold.

Not the end. The threshold. The specific moment between the career and whatever comes next, when the question of what comes next is no longer abstract because the career is no longer sufficient to defer it.

Most people stand at this threshold without a map. The career gave them everything except preparation for its absence. The structure that organized thirty-five years did not include instructions for what to do when the structure is gone. And so they stand there — competent, capable, accumulated, and uncertain — looking at a territory for which nothing in their professional life has prepared them.

This book is the map.

What the Sentence Produced

Before we move forward, let me name what the thirty-five years actually produced. Because this matters.

You are not arriving at the threshold empty. You are arriving with everything.

You have competence that cannot be faked
or fast-tracked. The kind that comes from
having done things under real conditions,
at real stakes, with real consequences,
over a long period of time. The kind that
knows the difference between the textbook
version of a problem and the version that
arrives on a Tuesday in bad weather with
the wrong people available and the metrics
running in real time on a screen
somewhere.

You have self-knowledge. Not the
performed self-knowledge of the workshop
or the coaching session but the actual kind
— the knowledge of how you perform
under pressure, what you reach for when
things go wrong, how you treat people
when the situation is difficult, what your
actual values are when the comfortable
abstractions are stripped away by
circumstances that require a real answer.

You have a network. Built over thirty-five
years of working alongside people,
delivering results, building reputation.
Many of these relationships have thinned.
Some have disappeared. But the
foundation is there, and foundations can be
rebuilt from.

And you have the specific, hard-won wisdom of someone who has been tested at length. Not theoretical wisdom. The kind that comes from having been wrong enough times to know what right looks like, and from having succeeded enough times to know the difference between luck and design.

The thirty-five years were not wasted. They were preparation.

The question is what they were preparation for.

That question is what the rest of this book answers.

The Threshold

You are standing at the end of something and the beginning of something else.

The something that is ending was real and earned and worth honoring. The something that is beginning is not yet defined, which is frightening, and is entirely yours, which is extraordinary.

Most people at this threshold are looking backward. At the career that is ending. At the identity that was built there. At the structure that organized everything and is now reorganizing itself without them at the center of it.

This book is going to ask you to turn around.

Not to dismiss what is behind you. To stop being organized by it. To face forward, toward the window that is open right now — the specific, time-limited, health-dependent, financially possible window that the next chapter will describe in detail.

The 35-year sentence is served.

What you do with the time that follows is the only question that matters now.

Turn the page.

CHAPTER TWO

The Retirement Trap

Someone I used to work with retired at sixty-three.

We had lunch the week before his last day. He was excited. Relieved. Twenty-eight years with the same company and he was finally done. He had the number. He had the plan. He had the speech prepared for the farewell party.

Six months later I ran into him at a coffee shop on a Tuesday morning. He looked different. Not older. Just smaller somehow. Like something had been removed and not replaced.

I asked how retirement was going.

"Great," he said. Too quickly.

Then a pause.

"I'm not sure what to do with myself, honestly."

I nodded. I ordered my coffee. I drove to the office.

But I kept thinking about that pause.

—

I was not headed for the same exit. Not by choice, anyway. The company had made that decision for me — the kind of corporate subtraction they dress up in language about restructuring and strategic realignment, as if the words make the math feel different. I was an expense. Expenses get managed. I got managed.

There is a word for this in Book Two of this series. I was Spat-Out.

But here is the thing about being Spat-Out that nobody tells you. It is clarifying.

When the corporate structure that organized your days, defined your identity, and told you what to do with your Monday mornings is suddenly gone, you find yourself standing in a very quiet room facing a very loud question.

What do I actually want?

Not what the job needed. Not what the org chart required. Not what the performance review measured. What did I — actual human being, with curiosity and skills and a finite number of mornings remaining — actually want from the rest of this life?

The honest answer surprised me.

More. I wanted more. More life and less work. More of the skills and experience I had spent decades building, applied to something that benefited my dream rather than someone else's quarterly numbers. I wanted to work harder than I ever had — but on my own terms, toward my own horizon, with the energy going somewhere that mattered to me.

I did not want to end up in that coffee shop on a Tuesday morning with the smaller look and the too-quick answer.

I wanted a different question entirely.

And then something else became clear. Something more urgent than ambition.

I thought about my colleague. His knees were bad. He moved carefully. He had mentioned over lunch that he and his wife had always planned to travel. Portugal, maybe. Or Japan. Somewhere they had never been. They had been saying that for twenty years.

I wondered if they would ever go.

I wondered if by the time the pension paperwork cleared and the grandchildren's schedules permitted and the doctor gave the all-clear, the version of them that could fully inhabit a foreign city — that could walk for three hours through a Lisbon neighborhood without planning it, that could take the late ferry and figure out dinner on the other side, that could be genuinely spontaneous and physically present in an unfamiliar place — would still be available.

I thought: that version of me is available right now.

Right now, while the curiosity is intact and the knees still work and the appetite for the unfamiliar is still sharp.

Right now, before age quietly renegotiates the terms of what is possible.

That thought became this book.

The Promise That Was Made

Let's start with what you were told.

Work hard. Stay loyal. Build your career. Save consistently. And at the end — sixty-five, maybe sixty-three if you were disciplined — you would arrive at retirement. The reward. The finish line. The decades you had earned by sacrificing the decades before them.

That was the deal.

Most people reading this book spent twenty, thirty, maybe forty years honoring that deal. You showed up. You performed. You deferred. You accumulated. You did what was asked.

The question this chapter is asking is simple.

Was the deal ever real?

The Three-Legged Stool Is Missing a Leg

Financial planners used to describe retirement security as a three-legged stool. The first leg was Social Security. The second was a pension from your employer. The third was personal savings.

It was a reasonable framework once.

It no longer describes reality.

The Social Security leg is wobbly. The Social Security Administration has been transparent about this for years. Without legislative changes, the trust fund is projected to be depleted by 2033, at which point benefits would be cut to approximately seventy-seven cents on the dollar. That is not a fringe prediction. That is the SSA's own number. The average monthly Social Security benefit in 2025 is approximately $1,907. For a couple, that might reach $3,000 to $3,800 per month if both partners qualify for full benefits. That is not a retirement. That is survival, in most American cities. And it assumes you wait until full retirement age to claim — which requires either the health to keep working or the savings to bridge the gap.

The pension leg has essentially disappeared. Private-sector defined benefit pension coverage fell from approximately 62% of workers in 1980 to roughly 16% by 2018. If you are reading this book, there is an 84% chance your employer never offered you a pension. The 401(k) replaced it — which means the employer transferred the investment risk, the management burden, and the uncertainty of outcome entirely onto you. You are not accumulating a guaranteed retirement income. You are managing a portfolio and hoping the math works out.

The personal savings leg is underfunded for most Americans. The median retirement savings for Americans between 55 and 64 is approximately

$185,000. At a standard 4% withdrawal rate, that generates $7,400 per year. Add average Social Security and you are looking at approximately $30,000 per year for a single person. In 2025, that is close to the federal poverty line for a family of four. It is not the retirement that was promised.

The three-legged stool, as currently constructed for most Americans, has one functional leg, one leg that has been sawed down to a stub, and one leg that was never properly built.

This is not a reason to despair. It is a reason to think differently.

The Cliff Edge Nobody Warned You About

Here is something the financial planning industry does not spend much time discussing.

The psychological architecture of traditional retirement is broken.

Traditional retirement is a cliff edge. You are employed — fully, structurally, with identity and purpose and daily forward motion — and then you are not. The calendar flips. The farewell party happens. The card gets signed. And then Monday morning arrives and the phone does not ring and the inbox does not fill and there is no meeting at nine and no deadline by Thursday and no reason that today needs to be different from yesterday.

The research on what happens next is not encouraging.

Studies consistently show elevated rates of depression, cognitive decline, and physical health deterioration in the years immediately following traditional retirement. A landmark Institute of Economic Affairs study found that full retirement increases the probability of clinical depression by 40% and increases the likelihood of having at least one diagnosed physical condition by 60%. These are not small effects. They are not statistical noise.

They are what happens when you remove the structure, purpose, social connection, identity, and forward momentum of a career — all at once — and replace it with leisure.

The human nervous system did not evolve for permanent leisure. It evolved for challenge, contribution, connection, and competence. The career, for all its frustrations, was delivering those things even when it felt like it was not. The Monday morning commute you resented was also the container that organized your day, your week, your year, your sense of yourself as someone who does things and matters to people.

When that container disappears, most people do not soar. Most people sit in coffee shops on Tuesday mornings wondering what to do with themselves.

My colleague was not unusual. He was typical.

The cliff edge does not discriminate. It catches the people who loved their careers and the people who hated them. It catches the well-prepared and the under-prepared. It catches the planners and the procrastinators. Because the problem is not financial. The problem is structural. And no amount of savings fixes a structural problem.

The FIRE Movement Got Half of It Right

Around 2010, a community of mostly younger people started noticing the same problems and deciding to solve them differently.

They called it FIRE. Financial Independence, Retire Early.

The insight was real. The standard career-until-sixty-five model was broken — not just financially but existentially. Why defer your entire life to a finish line that kept moving? Why spend your best decades in service of someone else's quarterly earnings report? The FIRE community did the math, realized it was solvable through aggressive savings and frugal living, and set about solving it.

The financial independence half of FIRE is genuinely useful. The 4% rule — build a portfolio equal to 25 times your annual expenses and withdraw 4% annually — forces a clarity most financial planning never delivers. What do you actually need to live? What would it cost to live it? How far are you from that number? These are the right questions. FIRE asked them out loud when mainstream financial culture was still telling everyone to trust the three-legged stool.

But the retire early half of FIRE has a documented failure mode.

The people who hit their number, quit their jobs, and expected freedom to feel like freedom frequently discovered something uncomfortable. They had solved the money problem. They had not solved the meaning problem.

Psychology Today drew on FIRE community accounts to name it plainly: financial independence removes money as an obstacle. It does not answer life's biggest questions. Many FIRE practitioners spent years fixating on the financial finish line without doing the internal work of figuring out who they wanted to be. When they arrived, they had no answer.

An INSEAD Business School study of post-financial-freedom individuals found that they often grappled with feelings of emptiness and anxiety, struggled to answer the question "what do you do now?", and found themselves in a constant search for labels to define their identity and purpose. They tried answers like "I'm an investor" or "I'm a full-time parent" or "I do nothing." None of them felt true or satisfying.

FIRE swapped burnout for boredom and called it a win.

Traditional retirement does the same thing at sixty-five that FIRE does at forty-two. It removes the structure without replacing it. It solves for the absence of work without designing for the presence of something better.

The Golden Gap is not FIRE. And it is not traditional retirement.

It is what happens when you take the financial independence insight seriously and add the design thinking that both movements forgot.

The Triangle

In The Leverage Code — Book One of this series — we mapped a framework that I want to return to here. It is the most honest description of the human life problem I know.

Three things a life requires: Health. Wealth. Time.

Not free time. Not time off. Time — the finite, non-renewable resource of a human life. The years you have left. The horizon.

The one thing that, once spent, cannot be earned back at any price.

You almost never have all three simultaneously.

When you are young, you have Health and Time. Your body works. Decades stretch ahead of you. The horizon feels infinite. But you have no Wealth. You are building it, trading the present for the promise of the future.

In your peak career years, you have Health and Wealth. Your body mostly cooperates. The money is finally real. The career is producing. But Time — the years remaining — is visibly shortening. You can feel it even if you do not say it out loud. The horizon is no longer infinite. Every year spent waiting for the next phase is a year that does not come back.

At traditional retirement age, you finally have Wealth and the freedom that was supposed to come with it. The career is done. But the Health vertex has started its decline. The body is less forgiving. And the Time vertex — the years remaining — has contracted dramatically. At sixty-five, the average American has approximately seventeen to twenty years ahead. At seventy, fewer. At seventy-five, fewer still. And those years are not equal. The early ones are the mobile ones. The capable ones. The ones in which the body can still carry you where you want to go.

Here is what the triangle shows you when you look at it honestly.

The alignment window — the specific period when all three vertices are simultaneously present in meaningful quantities — is not at sixty-five. It is not waiting patiently for you at the end of the career. It is happening right now, between roughly fifty and sixty-five, and it is shorter than you think.

Your Health is still substantially yours. Not the health of your thirties. But functional, capable, and — critically — still the kind of health that allows you to be fully present in the world. To walk. To explore. To be spontaneous. To recover from a long day and be ready for the next one.

Your Wealth is real. Accumulated through decades of career discipline. It may not be retirement-level wealth by traditional calculations. But it is gap-level wealth —

enough to fund a designed period of deliberate living while the rest of your financial life continues to work.

And your Time — the years remaining — is still enough to matter profoundly. The decisions you make in this window do not just affect the next year or two. They shape the decade that follows. They determine whether the later years are lived with the clarity, the health, and the sense of self that the Golden Gap builds — or with the quiet regret of a window that was open and not used.

Most people miss the alignment. Not because they are foolish. Because the script they were handed told them the alignment comes at sixty-five. By the time they discover it does not — that the health has already started to negotiate and the years remaining have already contracted — the window is narrowing.

The Golden Gap is the decision to use the window while all three vertices are still yours.

Not someday. Not when conditions are perfect. Not at sixty-five when the model says it is finally allowed.

Now.

Because Time — the real kind, the finite kind, the kind that does not come back — is the one vertex you cannot accumulate more of.

What the Career Is Doing to Your Body Right Now

Here is something nobody puts in the retirement planning conversation.

The career is not just consuming your time. It is consuming your body.

A writer who recently took a career sabbatical did something almost nobody does — he measured the physical impact of leaving. Not impressionistically. With biometric tracking, month by month, comparing the data before and after his last day at work.

The results were not subtle.

His resting heart rate dropped nearly ten beats per minute the moment the sabbatical began. Not gradually over weeks as the stress dissipated. Immediately. As though his nervous system had been waiting for permission to exhale and took it the instant the corporate structure disappeared.

His heart rate variability — the metric that measures how well the nervous system recovers from stress and adapts to demands — improved significantly. Higher heart rate variability means a body that is genuinely recovering between stressors rather than running continuously in the red.

His sleep quality improved. Despite sleeping in more than twenty different beds over four months — many of them uncomfortable by his own description — his body slept better in unfamiliar foreign accommodation than it had in his own bed at home.

His explanation for this is the most quietly devastating observation in the piece.

Maybe it felt like it finally had permission to rest.

He had been in the corporate workforce for roughly a decade.

Now do the math for someone who has been in the fast lane for thirty-five years.

The chronic stress markers he measured after ten years of working have been accumulating in you for three times as long. The heart rate elevation. The suppressed heart rate variability. The sleep quality erosion. The nervous system running continuously at a level it was never designed to sustain permanently.

None of this shows up dramatically on any given Tuesday. It shows up gradually, cumulatively, in the slow grinding down of a body that has been performing under sustained pressure for decades without a genuine break. Not a vacation — vacations do not move the biometric needle meaningfully because the nervous system knows you are going back. A genuine, structural removal of the stressor. The kind that only happens when the container that organized your stress finally comes down.

The Golden Gap is not just a financial decision or a lifestyle decision. It is a health decision. Possibly the most important health decision of your fifties.

This is not alarmism. It is data.

His step count also increased dramatically during his sabbatical — not because he started a new exercise program but because he was living in walkable cities and moving through the world on foot rather than sitting at a desk. Walking, wandering, exploring. He walked more in one month in Portugal than in any comparable period of his working life. No gym required. The environment did the work.

For the 50+ reader managing weight, blood pressure, cardiovascular health, or any of the chronic conditions that accumulate during a sedentary corporate career, this is not a trivial observation. The slow travel lifestyle — the daily walks through neighborhood markets, the cobblestone streets, the absence of a car and a parking lot and an elevator — is quietly and continuously better for your body than the suburban lifestyle it replaces.

And then there is what it does to your mind.

He described his emotional state before the sabbatical as driven by anxiety. Restless. Using distraction as a coping mechanism. Waking with anxiety in his chest two to three times a month. Spending evenings recovering from the day rather than building anything of his own.

After: driven by curiosity. Grounded. Addressing ideas instead of avoiding them. Experiencing emotions in real time rather than storing them for later.

The shift is not from unhappy to happy. It is more fundamental than that. It is from anxiety as fuel to curiosity as fuel. From reactive to intentional. From a life organized around escaping what needs to be escaped to a life organized around exploring what wants to be explored.

He names the most important insight plainly: a sabbatical is not the answer. It just spotlights it. None of his deep problems were resolved because he left. Putting himself on that path only showed him what his life looked like stripped down — and where to reinvent himself before suiting back up.

The Golden Gap does not solve your problems. It removes enough noise that your problems become visible — and therefore workable. It does not change who you are. It reveals who you already were, underneath everything the career put on top of you.

You will not return from the Golden Gap as a new person.

You will return as a clearer version of the one who left.

That person — it turns out — was always there. They just could not hear themselves think.

For someone who has spent thirty-five years storing emotions, deferring genuine self-knowledge, and performing under sustained pressure, that clarity is not just valuable.

It is necessary.

The Window

Ask anyone who has watched a parent's health decline what they wish their parent had done differently.

Almost no one says they wished their parent had worked an extra three years.

Almost everyone says some version of the same thing. I wish they had gone. I wish they had seen it. I wish they had not waited.

This is not a book about mortality. It is not designed to frighten you into action. But it would be dishonest not to name the truth that sits underneath every other argument in this chapter.

The version of you who can do this fully is available right now.

The version that can walk fifteen kilometers through a hillside town without planning it. That can take the overnight train and figure out where to sleep on the other side. That can sit in a foreign market for two hours watching ordinary life happen and feel completely at home in the strangeness of it. That can be spontaneous, physical, genuinely curious, and fully present in an unfamiliar place.

That version of you does not disappear overnight. But it changes — gradually and then more quickly — in ways that cannot be fully predicted or reversed. A knee. A diagnosis. A parent who needs care. An energy level that is simply not what it was.

Retirement is designed for old people. It assumes that the reward for a lifetime of work is rest — and that rest is best saved for the end, when you have finally accumulated enough years to justify it.

The Golden Gap is for people who are older but not yet old. Who understand the difference. Who recognize that the alignment of health, wealth, and time is not a permanent condition but a window — and that windows close.

This is not a fearful observation. It is a clarifying one.

Go now. While going is fully possible. While the curiosity is still sharp and the appetite for the unfamiliar is still real and the body that will carry you through a Portuguese village or a Vietnamese market or a Croatian ferry crossing at midnight is still the body you have always had.

Not because something terrible is coming.

Because something extraordinary is available right now.

What the Golden Gap Actually Is

Let me be precise, because the language matters.

The Golden Gap is not a vacation. A vacation is recovery from a life you return to unchanged. The Golden Gap changes the life you return to — or reveals that you are not returning to it at all.

The Golden Gap is not early retirement. Early retirement is a permanent exit from productive engagement with the world. The Golden Gap is a deliberate pause with a designed re-entry on entirely new terms. You are not stopping. You are redirecting.

The Golden Gap is not a gap year. That phrase belongs to twenty-two-year-olds and implies borrowed time from a life that has not yet started. The Golden Gap is claimed time — taken deliberately, from a life that is fully yours, at the specific moment when you have the most to bring to it.

The Golden Gap is not Spat-Out. Spat-Out is what happened to you. The Golden Gap is what you design in response. One is involuntary. The other is the most deliberate decision of your adult life. Book Two of this series helps you survive the hit. This book helps you build what the hit made possible.

Here is the definition.

The Golden Gap is the deliberately designed period of reset, exploration, and reinvention taken at the specific moment in your life when health, wealth, and time align — before age quietly renegotiates the terms of what is possible.

It is bounded but not rigid. It has a beginning designed with purpose and an exit designed with even more purpose. It may last six months, a year, two years. For some people it becomes the life itself — a permanent redesign rather than a temporary one. The duration matters less than the intention.

It is not defined by what you are leaving. It is defined by what you are building.

It is not organized around rest. It is organized around design — the deliberate construction of a life that is fully yours rather than the one you defaulted into.

And it is taken now. Not at sixty-five when the window has narrowed. Not when the grandchildren's schedules align and the doctor gives the all-clear and all the conditions are finally perfect.

Now. While the triangle is open.

What the Golden Gap Actually Costs

Let me make the financial case plainly because the fear of cost is what keeps most people in the trap.

The assumption baked into traditional retirement planning is that you need to accumulate enough to fund thirty years of retirement at your current lifestyle cost. For a couple spending $80,000 per year, that means a portfolio of approximately $2 million using the 4% rule. Most Americans are nowhere near that number at sixty-five — which is one reason the trap feels inescapable.

But here is what almost no financial planner will tell you.

Geographic arbitrage — living in places where a dollar goes significantly further — changes the math entirely.

Portugal is approximately 34% cheaper than the United States overall. Mexico is 50% to 70% cheaper. Southeast Asia runs 40% to 60% cheaper. Eastern Europe is 60% to 70% cheaper than its western counterpart. These are not estimates from travel blogs. They are documented, tracked, verified numbers from real people who have been living this way for years.

Two people who require $80,000 per year to live in suburban America may require $35,000 to $45,000 per year to live as well — better, actually, in terms of food quality, cultural richness, pace, and daily pleasure — in Lisbon, Medellín, or Chiang Mai.

But geographic arbitrage is only half the story. The other half is something most financial planners never name.

Call it the Convenience Premium.

During the career years, time was your scarce resource. Money bought it back. You paid someone to mow the lawn because you did not have time to mow the lawn. You ordered delivery because you did not have time to cook. You hired the cleaner because you did not have time to clean. Every dollar in that stack was spent not on a good or service but on the markup for not having to personally engage with it. The Convenience Premium — the annual total of everything a suburban couple spends specifically to buy back time — runs $12,000 to $17,000 per year.

Restaurant meals above home-cook cost. Food delivery fees. Grocery delivery markups. House cleaning. Lawn care. The full stack of outsourced domestic life.

The Golden Gap inverts the equation. Time is no longer scarce. The Convenience Premium does not just shrink. It largely disappears — not because you discipline yourself into austerity but because the life structure that generated the need for it no longer exists. There is no lawn. There is no car. The groceries are at a market you enjoy visiting. The cooking is not a chore. In a foreign city it is the culture.

The mindset shift is a single question, flipped. During the career: is this worth the time it saves? During the Golden Gap: is this worth the money it costs? Same transaction. Opposite question. Different answer almost every time.

One couple has documented five years of nomadic retirement across four continents and nineteen countries, tracking every dollar spent and publishing it publicly. Their average annual cost for two people: $28,050. Their most expensive year — which included a broken wrist, significant dental work, and the worst stock market performance since the 1930s — came in at $31,100. That is $85 per day for two people. In Europe. Eating well. Renting comfortable apartments. Traveling across eight countries and thirteen cities without once stepping foot in an airport.

Their portfolio, after five years of living on it, is approximately 20% larger than when they started. They have not earned a single dollar.

This is not magic. It is math. When your annual spend sits well below 4% of your portfolio, the remainder compounds. Geographic arbitrage, combined with the monthly rental strategy and a high-deductible insurance approach, creates a financial structure in which the Golden Gap costs significantly less than the suburban life you are currently funding — and frequently leaves your long-term financial position stronger than it would have been if you had stayed.

The Golden Gap does not require a retirement-sized portfolio. It requires a gap-sized portfolio — enough to fund one to two years of designed, deliberate living while the rest of your financial life continues to work.

For many readers of this book, that threshold is already met.

The trap is not that you cannot afford the Golden Gap. The trap is believing you cannot.

The Retirement Trap, Named

Traditional retirement is a trap not because retirement itself is wrong but because of the specific way it has been designed and delivered.

It arrives too late. The triangle is already tilting away from health by the time the wealth and time finally align.

It arrives all at once. The cliff edge — full employment to full leisure with no transition, no design, no preparation for who you will be without the title — is psychologically brutal for anyone whose identity was even partially built around career and contribution.

It is defined entirely by what it is not. Not working. Not commuting. Not answering to anyone. Not having to. The entire framework is organized around absence rather than presence. You are retiring from something. You are not, in any meaningful sense, arriving at something.

And it is sold as the destination when it is better understood as the final trap. The years spent accumulating for retirement are years spent in anticipatory mode — waiting for the life to start. The years of retirement itself are, for too many people, characterized by the slow discovery that the life they were waiting for was never clearly imagined and is therefore impossible to inhabit fully.

My colleague in the coffee shop was not unusual. He was typical.

The Golden Gap is the exit from the trap.

Not by refusing retirement. Not by pretending the career should last forever. But by refusing to let retirement be the first time you design your own life. By taking the alignment window when it opens. By building the transition deliberately rather than accepting the cliff edge. By arriving at the next phase as someone who has been doing the design work — not someone starting it at sixty-five in a coffee shop on a Tuesday morning, wondering what happened.

The Question That Changes Everything

Traditional retirement never asks the right question.

It asks: how much do you need? When can you stop? What is the number?

The Golden Gap asks something different.

What are you going toward?

Not what are you leaving. Not when can you stop. What does the life you actually want look like? What does a Tuesday in it feel like? Who are you when the job title is gone and the org chart no longer names you? What do you do with the curiosity that the career kept in a box for thirty years?

What would you build if you worked as hard as you ever have — but for yourself, toward your own horizon, with every bit of skill and experience and wisdom you have accumulated pointed at something that is purely, completely yours?

These are not retirement questions. They are design questions.

And they are the questions the Golden Gap is built to answer.

Not at sixty-five. Not when the health is declining and the window is narrowing and the version of you that could have done this fully is no longer quite available.

Now.

While the triangle is open. While the curiosity is sharp. While the body still works and the appetite for the unfamiliar is real and the ability to be fully present in a foreign city on a Tuesday morning — genuinely present, not just physically present — is still yours.

The Golden Gap is not the pause before your life resumes.

It is the moment your life becomes yours.

Five Honest Reflections

One: The retirement model most of us were sold was designed for a different economy, a different workforce, and a different life expectancy than the one we actually inhabit. Holding onto it is not prudent. It is just familiar.

Two: The FIRE community figured out that the standard script was broken. But solving for early financial escape without designing for arrival is not a solution. It is the same cliff edge at a younger age.

Three: The triangle is real. The alignment window is real. Most people miss it by waiting for a permission structure that never arrives.

Four: Retirement is for old people. The Golden Gap is for people who are older but not yet old. The difference is a window. The window is open right now.

Five: The question is not whether you can afford the Golden Gap. The question is whether you can afford to skip it.

CHAPTER THREE

The Movement Nobody Named

I was eating breakfast.

We had been in Australia for a few weeks by then — staying at a friend's house while he was away traveling, living in a quiet suburb, settling into the specific calm of a life that had no schedule and no inbox and no one waiting for a deliverable by Thursday. My wife had put her job on hold. My job was gone. We had spent two weeks at home before leaving, working through a list that started at fifteen companies to call and became thirty, clearing the decks, locking the house, leaving the bowl and spoon on the kitchen island so it would not look abandoned.

We were doing a thing. We just did not know what to call it yet.

The morning show was on. I was only half-watching — the kind of passive morning television that fills space without demanding attention. And then a woman from a travel company came on to discuss something she called the Golden Gap Year. For retirees.

I looked at my wife.

She looked at me.

I said: we are on a Golden Gap right now.

Not a retirement. We were not retired. My departure from the career had not been my choice, and my wife was taking a pause rather than an exit. But what we were doing — the reset, the deliberate pause, the choosing of the life over the job — was exactly what the woman on the television was describing for a different audience at a different life stage.

I picked up my phone and searched for the phrase. Two or three relevant results. Mostly destination guides. Mostly about how to position retirement savings. Nothing about the psychological architecture of the decision. Nothing about what it actually felt like. Nothing about the couple in their fifties who needed a gap not because they were retired but because they were human beings who had been running at full speed for thirty-five years and needed to stop — deliberately, intentionally, with a plan — and figure out what came next.

I opened my laptop.

I never expected to write a book. But
something needed to be written. Because
what I was beginning to understand,
sitting in that quiet suburb in Australia
with no schedule and no deliverable and a
morning show playing in the background,
was that this thing we were doing was not
unusual. It was not pioneering. It was not
even particularly original.

It was everywhere. It just did not have a
name.

—

The Movement That Already Exists

Here is something that most people
planning a Golden Gap do not know.

They are not the first.

Not by a long way.

The movement they are joining — the
deliberate, designed, post-career pause for
people over fifty who have accumulated
enough to do it — is already one of the
largest lifestyle shifts in modern history. It
is happening on four continents
simultaneously, under different names,
with different vehicles, through different

communities. It is happening in Australian caravans and Lisbon apartments and Chiang Mai coworking spaces and Airbnb monthly rentals in Medellín. It is happening in Reddit communities and Facebook groups and private blogs and at dinner tables in foreign cities where two people who have been together for twenty-five years are discovering that they have, finally, something new to talk about.

The movement has no single name because it arrived from multiple directions at once. Different communities named their version of it differently. But they are all describing the same essential phenomenon: the deliberate use of the window between a career and whatever comes next by people who have accumulated enough to use it intentionally.

The interest in living or retiring abroad has grown from 4% of Americans in the 1970s to 17% today — with 26% of current retirees considering moving abroad and 35% of future retirees indicating they plan to do so. That is not a fringe tendency. That is a structural shift in how an entire generation is thinking about the second half of life.

In 2024-2025, retirees accounted for 62% of US citizens relocating abroad. Over 760,000 Americans are already receiving their Social Security payments in foreign countries. The Great American Retirement Exodus — as one 2025 research report named it — is not a future trend. It is a present reality.

And it is accelerating.

The Adjacent Movements — Each One Getting Part of It Right

The Golden Gap did not emerge from nowhere. It is the synthesis of several adjacent movements that each identified part of the problem and built partial solutions.

The Grey Nomads

In Australia, they have had a name for this for decades.

A grey nomad is someone aged fifty-five or over who travels for extended periods — months, sometimes years — independently, usually in a caravan or motorhome, exploring the country at a pace that tourism cannot replicate. Estimates suggest that 20% of grey nomads live the nomadic travelling lifestyle for more than two years. They see this adventure as a way of life, a reward to themselves after a working life contributing to social and economic systems.

By 2021, more than 750,000 recreational vehicles were registered in Australia, with 29% of domestic camping and caravanning trips made by people aged fifty-five and over. At any given time, an estimated 30,000 to 40,000 grey nomads are living on the road across Australia — a number that grows every year as the baby boomer generation moves through retirement age.

The grey nomad movement got something fundamentally right: that the post-career years are not the end of adventure but the beginning of it. That health and time, briefly aligned, create a window that should be used rather than watched from a front porch. That the vehicle of the gap matters less than the intention behind it.

What the grey nomad model is missing — for the international Golden Gap reader — is the geographic scope. The caravan stays in Australia. The Golden Gap reader wants the world.

The FIRE Community

Financial Independence Retire Early. Millions of mostly younger people who figured out, largely independently, that the standard career-until-sixty-five model was broken and set about solving the financial dimension of the problem with extraordinary discipline.

I found them on Reddit. I had been doing my own research, reading about what people did after they hit their financial independence number. The FIRE communities are large, sophisticated, and genuinely useful on the money side. The 4% rule. The Roth conversion ladder. Geographic arbitrage. They have done the math and documented it thoroughly.

But I noticed something when I read through the threads. When someone in the FIRE community hit their number — the portfolio target that was supposed to unlock freedom — they frequently did not know what to do next. The posts about what to do after FIRE were more uncertain than the posts about how to achieve it. The spreadsheets were detailed and confident. The identity question was vague and uncomfortable.

I asked in one community what people planned to do with their freedom once they had it. I got some awkward responses. A few genuinely interesting ideas. But mostly I noticed that the question itself felt slightly out of place — as though the point of FIRE was the achievement of the number, and the life that followed was a detail to be worked out later.

This is the FIRE movement's partial answer. It solved the wealth vertex of the triangle. It left the time and identity vertices largely unaddressed.

The Golden Gap is FIRE plus the question FIRE forgot to ask.

The Slow Travel Community

Across Reddit and the travel blogosphere, a quieter community has been building for years. Not retirees, not FIRE adherents — people of all ages who discovered that inhabiting a place for a month is categorically different from visiting it for a week.

The slow travel community understood something the mainstream travel industry has no commercial interest in acknowledging: the tourist experience is designed around the sale of novelty, and novelty is subject to the law of diminishing returns. The seventh temple produces less feeling than the first. Moving fast through a checklist of highlights is not travel — it is consumption.

Slow travel community members talk about the four-week minimum — the threshold at which a city stops being somewhere you are visiting and starts being somewhere you live. They talk about base camps, about regional day trips, about the market vendor who recognizes your face, about the coffee shop where they know your order. They talk about the specific, irreplaceable pleasure of having something to tell each other over dinner that neither of you saw coming.

A third of Australian seniors have embraced slow travel, extending their visits to experience places more deeply. This is not a fringe preference. It is the discovery, by people old enough to know the difference, that depth produces more than speed.

The slow travel community got the philosophy right. What it has not done — at least not consistently — is connect the philosophy to the specific life stage of the 50+ reader: the person with the resources to do it properly, the health to do it fully, and the window of time that will not always be available.

The Digital Nomads — Aging Up

The digital nomad movement is fifty million people strong globally and growing. Millennials still dominate at 37% to 38% of the community, but perhaps most surprisingly, 14% of nomads are fifty-five or older. This age diversity reflects a fundamental shift in how people view work and life balance. Seasoned professionals are increasingly choosing location independence over corner offices.

The Baby Boomer segment of the digital nomad community — 6% to 9% of the total — is the fastest-growing age cohort in the movement. These are not young people on adventure breaks. They are experienced professionals who have discovered that the combination of accumulated skills, geographic arbitrage, and the infrastructure of the slow travel life creates a financial and experiential model that is simply better than the one they left.

The digital nomad movement gave the world the infrastructure. The visa programs, the coworking spaces, the monthly rental platforms, the eSIM providers, the international banking solutions. All of it was built for a younger demographic and all of it is available to the 50+ Golden Gap reader who knows where to look.

The Infrastructure Is Already Built

This is the part that surprised me most when I started looking.

The Golden Gap is not a radical idea requiring pioneer logistics. The infrastructure is already there — built by and for the adjacent movements that arrived first, now available to the 50+ reader who is arriving with more resources, more self-knowledge, and more deliberate intention than any of the earlier arrivals.

More than seventy countries now offer some form of digital nomad visa or extended stay permit. Portugal's D7 visa. Greece's remote worker program. Panama's Pensionado. France's VLS-T long-stay visitor visa. Croatia, Georgia,

Thailand, Colombia — the list grows every year as countries recognize the economic value of attracting people who spend local but earn globally.

The accommodation market has restructured around monthly stays. Airbnb's monthly discount feature — 40% to 50% cheaper than nightly rates — was built for this population. The furnished apartment industry in Lisbon, Chiang Mai, Medellín, and every other major slow travel hub is now explicitly competing for the monthly tenant with good WiFi, a real kitchen, and a comfortable bed.

The international insurance market has produced products specifically for the long-term nomadic traveler — not vacation travel insurance that caps out at forty-five days, but catastrophic coverage policies designed for continuous international residence.

The banking infrastructure — Schwab's global ATM reimbursement, Wise's mid-market currency conversion, Revolut's international transfers — was built by financial technology companies that saw this population forming and built products for it.

Software tools now exist specifically for the 50+ slow traveler. Planning tools that market explicitly to retirees and digital nomads, offering itinerary management, budget tracking, and Schengen compliance monitoring. Someone built a business around this. That is not a hobby project. That is market validation.

The movement is large enough that someone built software for it.

What the Numbers Actually Show

Let me put some scale on this.

Recent polls show about a third of Americans — around 117 million people — would like to go and settle in another country. A concept that once felt out there, limited to budget travelers or serious adventurers, is now squarely in the mainstream.

As of 2024 there were 5.4 million Americans living abroad, of which 23% were over 65 — approximately 1.26 million Americans of retirement age living outside the United States. That number has grown steadily every year since 2018 and continues to accelerate.

In Australia, nearly two in five seniors reported taking their last big holiday in the past year — a significant jump from less than one in five in 2022. More than two in five Australian seniors believe creating travel memories is more important than leaving a financial inheritance.

A third of Australian seniors have embraced slow travel, extending their visits to experience places more deeply.

The digital nomad population globally now exceeds fifty million people, with the over-fifty-five segment the fastest-growing age cohort in the movement.

These are not small numbers. These are the numbers of a mass movement that arrived before anyone named it and built an entire infrastructure while the mainstream culture was still insisting that retirement meant a rocking chair and a predictable schedule.

The Golden Gap is not a radical departure from the mainstream. It is the mainstream — it just has not been named yet.

What the Golden Gap Names That the Others Could Not

Here is why the adjacent movements, for all their genuine value, left a gap that this book addresses.

The grey nomad movement is geographically domestic and vehicle-dependent. It is specifically Australian in its cultural formation and its domestic scope. For the American or British or Canadian reader, the grey nomad is an inspiration but not a template.

The FIRE community solved the financial equation but left the identity question and the design question largely unaddressed. It is also primarily a younger person's movement — the 50+ reader who did not save aggressively from age twenty-five cannot fast-track to the FIRE number. But they may already be at or near a gap-sized portfolio without knowing it.

The slow travel community has the philosophy right but has not organized around the specific needs and resources of the 50+ reader. It skews younger, more adventurous in the backpacker sense, and less systematic about the financial and health preparation that makes the gap sustainable for someone who has been in a career for thirty-five years.

The digital nomad movement has the infrastructure right but is organized primarily around work — around continuing to generate income while traveling. The Golden Gap reader is often in a different position: they have accumulated enough to pause, to explore, to design — without needing to immediately replace their income from a foreign city.

The Golden Gap synthesizes what each of these movements got right and adds what each was missing:

The grey nomad's understanding that the post-career years are for adventure, not decline.

The FIRE community's financial discipline and its portfolio math.

The slow travel community's philosophy of depth over speed, presence over collection, the monthly stay over the three-day highlight reel.

The digital nomad movement's practical infrastructure — the visas, the banking, the accommodation platforms, the connectivity.

And to all of it, the Golden Gap adds the specific ingredient that none of the adjacent movements fully address: the deliberate design of the identity that comes after the career. Not just the logistics of leaving. The architecture of what you are building.

You Are Not a Pioneer. You Are the Latest Arrival.

The woman on the morning show was talking to retirees. The travel company she represented was packaging itineraries for people who had finished their careers and were looking for someone to organize the adventure.

That is a version of the Golden Gap. It is not the full version.

The full version is not a package tour. It is not a curated itinerary with a guide and a group and a schedule that someone else designed.

The full version is the deliberate, personal, specifically yours design of the period between your career and whatever comes next — taken at the moment when the triangle is aligned, with the resources you have built, at the pace that serves your actual life rather than someone else's product.

Millions of people are already doing this. The grey nomads in their caravans. The FIRE adherents in their Lisbon apartments. The slow travelers extending their stays to four weeks, then six, then indefinitely. The Baby Boomer digital nomads discovering that the infrastructure built for millennials works perfectly well for someone with more resources, more self-knowledge, and thirty-five years of accumulated capability.

You are not a pioneer.

You are the latest arrival to a movement that has been building for decades. The movement just needed a name.

This is the Golden Gap.

Welcome.

CHAPTER FOUR

Who Takes the Golden Gap

People arrive at the Golden Gap from different directions.

Some did not choose to arrive at all. The company made the choice for them — the restructuring, the redundancy, the role that evaporated while they were still performing it well. They are standing at the threshold not because they planned to be there but because the career ended before they did.

Some chose to arrive before it was done to them. They could see the burnout coming — the Sunday dread, the diminishing returns on effort, the version of themselves that was getting smaller and more depleted with each passing year — and they decided to leave before the leaving was involuntary. They chose the threshold rather than being pushed to it.

Some planned their arrival for years. They ran the numbers, built the portfolio, had the conversations, made the preparations, and then — when the conditions were right — they walked through the door they had been building toward for a decade. The most organized of arrivals. The least surprised.

Some arrived as a couple, both at the inflection point simultaneously, trying to answer the question of what comes next for us rather than for me. The gap as the relationship redesign as much as the life redesign.

Some arrived alone — solo, divorced, or widowed — and discovered that the specific freedom of designing for one was not a consolation but a gift. The gap shaped entirely around one person's actual preferences, with no negotiation required.

And some arrived knowing exactly what they were going to make. Not knowing yet whether it would work. But knowing what direction they were pointed in and choosing the gap as the time and space to build it.

Six types. One window. Countless individual stories that do not fit neatly into any of the categories because human lives are always messier than taxonomies. But the types are recognition devices, not definitions. If you read one and think that

is close enough, the chapter has done its
job.

Type One — The Spat-Out

The Spat-Out did not plan this.

The role disappeared. The restructuring
came with their name on it. The company
that had organized their professional
identity for twenty years decided, in a
meeting they were not invited to, that the
math no longer included them.

This is Book Two territory — the Spat-Out
experience is the subject of the second
book in this series. But the Spat-Out reader
arrives at the Golden Gap through a
specific version of the threshold. They did
not choose the exit. What they choose now
is what to do with it.

And here is the thing about the Spat-Out
that nobody tells them in the immediate
aftermath of the exit: the involuntary
departure is frequently the best thing that
ever happened to them. Not because the
experience is painless — it is not. The
identity loss, the financial anxiety, the
specific grief of having something you built

removed by people who did not build it —
all of that is real and takes time to process.

But the Spat-Out has something the other
types often lack. Clarity.

When the career ends without your
permission, the question of what comes
next cannot be deferred. You cannot push
it to next year or wait until the conditions
are perfect. The question is present and
immediate and will not be managed by
staying busy. You are forced to face it —
and facing it, honestly and directly, is the
beginning of the design work that the
Golden Gap requires.

The Spat-Out reader often discovers,
somewhere in the weeks after the exit, that
the thing they thought the career was
giving them — the identity, the purpose,
the forward motion — was already eroding
before the end. The role was consuming
them. The metrics were getting more
invasive. The work was less meaningful
than it had been. The exit, for all its
trauma, removed them from something
that was also removing them.

The Spat-Out arrives at the Golden Gap
already through the hardest part. The

threshold was crossed for them. Now the design work begins.

Type Two — The Burned Out

The Burned Out is still employed.

This is the uncomfortable truth about this type. They are still showing up, still performing, still delivering results that the metrics confirm and the performance reviews endorse. From the outside they are fine. From the inside they are running on the last reserves of something that does not replenish the way it used to.

The Burned Out knows the Sunday feeling. The specific quality of Sunday evening dread that is not about anything in particular — not a difficult Monday task or a problematic meeting — but about the simple fact of Monday. Of the week beginning again. Of doing what they have been doing, again, for another week, toward an outcome that feels less and less worth the cost.

The Burned Out also knows the diminishing returns. Work that once produced satisfaction now produces merely completion. Problems that once felt interesting now feel like noise. The career has not changed dramatically — the Burned Out has. They have been running at full speed for long enough that the speed itself has become the problem.

The Burned Out chooses the gap before the gap is chosen for them.

This is an act of self-preservation that takes more courage than it appears to from outside. The Burned Out is giving up something real — income, structure, professional identity, the forward motion of a career that still has runway — in exchange for something they cannot yet fully name. They are leaving something known and functional for something unknown and undesigned.

What they are leaving is a career that is still working in every external sense. What they are running toward is the version of themselves that the career has been slowly consuming.

The Burned Out is one of the most common types of Golden Gap reader. They are also the type who faces the most skepticism from people around them — because they are leaving from a position that looks, from the outside, like success. The people who love them often cannot understand why they would walk away from something that appears to be working.

The answer is that it is working for everything except the person doing it. And that is not, ultimately, an acceptable trade.

Type Three — The Ready

The Ready saw this coming.

They have been reading about geographic arbitrage for three years. They have a spreadsheet. They know their 4% number and they know how close they are to it. They have had the conversations with their financial advisor, made the appropriate adjustments to their account structure, begun the Roth conversion ladder. They have read the slow travel blogs and identified their first base camp and calculated the monthly cost of living in four candidate cities.

The Ready is the most organized arrival at the Golden Gap and often the most underestimated one.

People assume the Ready is playing it safe — that the preparation is a form of procrastination, a way of staying in the planning phase indefinitely rather than taking the actual leap. Sometimes this is true. Sometimes The Ready needs someone to tell them that no amount of additional preparation will eliminate the uncertainty, and that the gap begins when you decide it begins rather than when all conditions are optimal.

But more often The Ready has simply done what people who take the long view always do. They identified the window. They prepared for it. They arrived at it with their eyes open and their affairs in order.

The Ready tends to have the smoothest gap — not because the gap itself is easier but because the preparation was thorough. The home decision was made deliberately and early. The financial structure was optimized before departure. The health sprint was completed without rushing. The digital infrastructure was tested before it was needed. The first base camp was chosen with care rather than booked in a panic.

The Ready often struggles to explain to people around them why they are leaving when everything is going so well. The answer — which the Ready has usually arrived at through years of honest reflection — is that going well and going right are not the same thing. The career was going well. The Golden Gap is going right.

Type Four — The Couple at a Crossroads

The Couple at a Crossroads is not one person making a decision. It is two people arriving at the same threshold from slightly different directions, at slightly different speeds, with slightly different fears and slightly different visions of what the other side looks like.

This is one of the most complex types because it requires two sets of answers to align, or at least to find enough overlap to move forward together. One partner may be more ready than the other. One may have financial concerns that the other does not share. One may be energized by the prospect of unstructured time while the other finds it quietly terrifying. One may have a vision of what the gap looks like that is recognizably different from the other's vision.

The Couple at a Crossroads has to design
not just a gap but a shared gap. Which is
both more challenging and more rewarding
than designing one alone.

The gap is frequently the most intimate
period of a long relationship. When the
parallel lives of employed partnership —
separate offices, separate commutes,
separate days — collapse into shared time
in a foreign city, everything that was
managed by structure is suddenly visible.
The differences are clearer. The
compatibility is also clearer. The gap strips
the relationship down to its actual
condition rather than its managed one.

This can be frightening. It is also, for most
couples who navigate it with honesty, one
of the best things that ever happened to
them. The separate outings. The download
conversation at dinner. The version of each
other that emerges when there is finally
time and space and something new to talk
about.

The Couple at a Crossroads often arrives at
the Golden Gap as two people who love
each other and know each other well and
are about to discover things about each

other — and about themselves — that the career years never allowed.

That is not a risk to be managed. It is a feature of the gap that the career could never provide.

Type Five — The Solo Redesigner

The Solo Redesigner is doing this for one.

They are single, or divorced, or widowed. The gap they are designing has no second person to negotiate with, no partner's timeline to accommodate, no shared budget to balance against competing visions. The base camp is chosen by one person's preferences. The daily rhythm is calibrated to one person's needs. The adventure is pointed in whatever direction one person finds most interesting.

This can sound lonely. It is sometimes lonely. The Solo Redesigner knows this and has made the calculation that the specific freedom of designing for one is worth the specific challenge of doing it alone.

What the Solo Redesigner discovers, almost universally, is that slow travel is one of the most social lifestyles available. The monthly base camp, the local market, the language class, the cooking class, the photography walk with the local guide — all of these create the conditions for genuine connection that the suburban life they left often did not. The Solo Redesigner who arrives in Lisbon or Chiang Mai or Medellín for a month and stays in a walkable neighborhood finds that they are far less alone than they expected.

The Solo Redesigner is also free to pivot in ways that partnered gap-takers cannot. If the base camp city does not feel right, they move. If the phase runs long or short, they adjust without negotiation. If an unexpected opportunity appears — a conversation that becomes a collaboration, a city that reveals itself as somewhere they want to stay, a direction that was not on the original plan — they can follow it.

The Solo Redesigner is often the most agile type of gap-taker. Agility is not nothing. It is frequently the thing that makes the gap into what it needs to be rather than what it was planned to be.

Type Six — The Maker

The Maker arrives at the Golden Gap knowing what they are going to make.

Not knowing yet whether it will work. Not knowing whether the income will come, whether the market will find it, whether the thing being made will find its audience or its purpose or its form. But knowing the direction. Knowing that the work is real. Knowing that the alternative — returning to a career structure that was consuming everything in exchange for a salary and a title — is no longer acceptable.

The Maker is writing books that do not yet have many sales. The Maker is building a consulting practice that is not yet at career income. The Maker is developing a creative business that is still in its early, uncertain, unconfirmed phase. The Maker is doing the work of building something that is entirely theirs — every hour of effort going toward their own horizon rather than someone else's quarterly numbers.

The Maker is not necessarily positioned for traditional retirement. This is important to say plainly, because the Maker type is often left out of the retirement-travel conversation precisely because they do not fit the profile of someone who has accumulated enough to stop. The Maker has a runway. Maybe a short one. Maybe one they are extending through careful financial management and geographic arbitrage while the thing being made develops.

But the Maker has something more valuable than a full retirement portfolio. They have a direction.

The gap for the Maker is not the exploration phase — the direction is already clear. The gap is the deliberate creation of the time and space to build the next thing without the career consuming all available resources. It is the calculated bet that the work is worth the runway it requires. It is the specific courage of someone who knows what they are making and has decided to make it.

I am making time, to make a plan, to make something.

That is the Maker's definition of the Golden Gap. It is also — if you look at it clearly — the most ambitious version of the gap available. The Maker is not resting. They are not exploring. They are not decompressing. They are doing the hardest and most intentional work of their professional life, finally, on their own terms.

The subtitle of this book is Reclaim, Reset, and Reposition Your Life After 50. The Maker is doing all three simultaneously. Reclaiming the time the career consumed. Resetting from anxiety as fuel to curiosity as fuel. Repositioning everything — the skills, the experience, the accumulated capability of thirty-five years — toward something that is genuinely theirs.

The Maker is not the easiest type to be. The validation does not come from a performance review or a quarterly metric. The reward is not a salary deposited on a predictable schedule. The Maker is working on faith — not blind faith, but the specific earned faith of someone who knows their capabilities, trusts their direction, and is willing to do the work while the work does its work.

The book sales come later. The practice builds. The thing being made takes its shape. But only if the Maker keeps making.

The Thread That Connects Them

Six types. Six different routes to the same threshold.

The Spat-Out did not choose the exit but chose the response. The Burned Out chose the exit before the exit chose them. The Ready chose it years ago and arrived prepared. The Couple at a Crossroads chose it together and are navigating the shared design. The Solo Redesigner chose it alone and is discovering that alone is not the same as lonely. The Maker chose it for the work and is betting everything on the direction.

What connects all six is not a financial profile. Not a life circumstance. Not a personality type or a risk tolerance or a particular kind of courage.

What connects them is the moment of recognition.

The moment when the window became visible — when the alignment of health and wealth and time was not just a theoretical framework but a felt reality, present and finite and right now. The moment when the gap stopped being something people like that do and became something I could do. Something I need to do. Something that, if

I do not do it now, I may not be able to do the same way later.

That moment is the beginning of the Golden Gap regardless of which type you are.

The question is not which type you belong to. The question is whether you recognize the window.

And whether you are ready to walk through it.

—

A question before you continue:

Which of these six types are you? You may be more than one — most people are a combination, with one type dominant and another running alongside it. The Spat-Out who became the Maker. The Burned Out who is also The Ready. The Couple at a Crossroads where one partner is The Ready and the other is The Burned Out.

Name your type. Write it down if that helps. The rest of this book is written for all six — but knowing which one you are will help you find the chapters that speak most directly to your specific situation.

Your type is the beginning of your design.

CHAPTER FIVE

What a Gap Actually Is

I had put in for two weeks of vacation starting the first week of March.

The plan was clear enough. Take the time. Go to Australia. See my wife's family, walk the places we had loved when we were dating twelve years ago, get the mental space I had been running out of. And somewhere in those two weeks, make the decision I had been building toward: resign. Start the next thing. Stop trading my time for someone else's outcomes and start building something that was mine.

The position was eliminated at the end of January.

The plan changed. The direction did not.

What happened next was not a vacation. It was not early retirement — we are not retired and the next chapter is not a cessation of work but a different relationship with it. It was not a sabbatical — a sabbatical implies a return to the same thing, and returning to the same thing was the one outcome we were deliberately not designing for. It was not the young-person gap year — we met twelve years ago, later in life than most, and what we are building together is not a break before the career resumes but the permanent restructured version of the life we want.

It was something specifically its own.

Two months in Australia. Then home, still creating, still building, still making — generating the first threads of income from work that was ours rather than someone else's. Then the road, the base camps, the slow travel life that supplements savings and builds toward something sustainable. Not a temporary pause. A permanent redesign.

That is the Golden Gap.

Not the theory of it. The lived version of it, arriving ahead of schedule, larger and more intentional than the two weeks originally planned, shaped by what we needed rather than what we had planned.

—

Last night at dinner we met a couple.

He is American, mid-twenties, works in hospitality. Good at it. Made real money as a server in the US — the kind of hourly rate that builds savings fast when you are young and disciplined. The new no-tax-on-tips legislation gave him an extra $3,500 back on his 2025 taxes. He met a Serbian girl in Hawaii. They fell in love. Her visa ran out. They flew to Japan for two weeks — the cleanest country he had ever seen, he said — then Manila, which was the dirtiest city he had ever seen, then Bali for a week, then Australia on a work-and-holiday visa. Four months here, then Eastern Europe, working jobs as they go to fund the next leg.

It is a magnificent way to be twenty-five.

It is not the Golden Gap.

Not because their version is wrong — it is completely right for who they are and where they are. But because what they are doing is different from what this book is about in almost every dimension that matters. They are chasing the next visa and the next cash job. They are moving fast between dramatic contrasts — Japan to Manila, clean to chaotic, familiar to completely foreign. They are funded by hospitality hours and tax refunds and the specific resourcefulness of people who have not yet accumulated much and therefore have nothing to protect.

The Golden Gap reader is at a different place in the same life. They have accumulated. They have history — with a career, with a partner, with a set of skills that took decades to build. They have the specific resource that the young couple at dinner does not yet have: enough. Not infinite, but enough. Enough to design deliberately rather than improvise continuously. Enough to choose the base camp rather than the next cheap flight. Enough to inhabit a place rather than pass through it.

The contrast is useful. It shows, more clearly than any definition, what the Golden Gap is not.

What a Gap Is Not

Not a vacation. A vacation is recovery from a life you return to unchanged. You go somewhere, you rest or explore or do whatever the vacation is for, and then you come back. The life resumes. The job is there on Monday. The structure that organized everything before you left organizes everything after you return. The Golden Gap changes the life you return to — or reveals, as it frequently does, that you are not returning to the old version of it at all. The gap is not the interruption of your life. It is the redesign of it.

Not early retirement. Early retirement, as the FIRE community defines it, is a permanent exit from productive engagement. You have accumulated enough. You stop. The accumulated portfolio takes over the work of generating income. The career is finished. The Golden Gap is not finished. The Maker is building. The Burned Out is resetting before the next thing. The Ready is exploring before deciding what the next chapter looks like. Even the Spat-Out, whose career ended without their permission, is not finished — they are repositioning. The Golden Gap is a deliberate pause with a designed re-entry on entirely new terms. Not stopping. Redirecting.

Not a sabbatical. A sabbatical is a temporary leave from a position you plan to return to. The professor takes a sabbatical to research and write, then returns to the department. The structure is intact. The relationship is intact. The re-entry is planned and expected. The Golden Gap does not assume re-entry to the same

thing. It assumes re-entry to something —
but what that something is gets designed
during the gap rather than assumed before
it. The Golden Gap is the sabbatical where
the return destination is unknown at
departure. That is not a flaw in the design.
It is the design.

Not the young-person gap year. The gap
year of the twenty-two-year-old is
borrowed time from a life that has not yet
started. The Golden Gap is claimed time
from a life that is fully formed and fully
owned. The person taking it at fifty-five has
built the resources, the self-knowledge,
and the specific capability that makes the
gap genuinely productive rather than
merely exploratory. The twenty-two-year-
old is figuring out who to be. The fifty-five-
year-old already knows — and is finally,
deliberately, using that knowledge for
themselves.

Not Spat-Out. Spat-Out is what happened
to you. The Golden Gap is what you design
in response. One is involuntary. The other
is the most deliberate decision of your
adult life. This distinction matters even for
the Spat-Out type. The moment of exit may
have been involuntary. The moment of

deciding what to do with the exit — that moment is yours. The gap begins when you claim it, not when the company ends your employment.

Not the hustle version of digital nomadism. The American server and the Serbian girl are doing something real and brave and adventurous. But they are also, in a specific way, still running — chasing the next visa, the next job, the next city, the next way to fund the leg after this one. The Golden Gap is not organized around continuous income generation as a survival requirement. It is organized around deliberate design — the gap-sized portfolio providing the runway while the next thing is built, the geographic arbitrage reducing the burn rate, the pace set by intention rather than by financial necessity. The digital nomad hustle is magnificent at twenty-five. At fifty-five, with accumulated resources and a specific direction, it is not the model. The Golden Gap has a runway. The runway is what makes the design possible.

The Three Words

The subtitle of this book is

Reclaim. The career consumed things. Time. Energy. Headspace. The curiosity that used to chase ideas for the pleasure of the chase. The friendships that thinned because the schedule never aligned. The health that the desk and the stress and the twelve-hour days were quietly degrading. The version of yourself that existed before the career organized everything around its own requirements. The Golden Gap reclaims these things. Not all at once. Not completely. But the decompression phase — the first weeks and months when the nervous system is releasing thirty-five years of accumulated pressure — is the beginning of the reclamation. The heart rate drops. The sleep deepens. The curiosity box opens. The things that were consumed start to come back. Reclaim is the first word because it is the first work of the gap. Before you can reset or reposition, you have to recover what the career took.

Reset. The career ran on a specific operating system. Anxiety as fuel. The inbox that organized the day. The meeting that structured the week. The performance review that defined the year. The approval architecture of an organization that told you, continuously, whether you were succeeding or failing by its standards. The Golden Gap installs a different operating system. Curiosity as fuel. The day organized around what is interesting rather than what is urgent. The week shaped by what needs to be built rather than what needs to be delivered. This upgrade does not happen automatically. It requires the specific conditions of the gap — the time, the space, the removal of the old operating system's demands — to complete. The reset is not a decision. It is a process. But when it is running, the difference is unmistakable. Anxiety as fuel produces a life organized around escaping what needs to be escaped. Curiosity as fuel produces a life organized around exploring what wants to be explored. The Golden Gap is the transition between the two.

Reposition. The thirty-five years of the career were not wasted. They were preparation. The skills, the self-knowledge, the network, the hard-won wisdom of someone who has been tested at length — all of it is available and intact at the threshold of the Golden Gap. What changes is where it is pointed. Repositioning means taking everything the career built and directing it toward the life you are designing rather than the organization you were serving. The operational expertise applied to building your own practice. The management capability applied to managing your own creative process. The problem-solving instinct applied to problems you actually care about. The Maker repositions most explicitly — the gap is literally the space in which the skills of the career are redirected toward the thing being built. But all six types reposition in their own way.

Reclaim. Reset. Reposition.

In that order. Because you cannot reset what you have not reclaimed. And you cannot reposition toward something new until the reset is complete.

The Spectrum

The Golden Gap is not one thing.

It runs on a spectrum from a focused six-month reset to a complete and permanent life redesign that never fully ends.

At the shorter end: six to twelve months. A deliberate pause with a specific intention — to decompress, to decide, to rebuild health, to launch a project, to reconnect with a partner, to take the trip that has been on the list for eleven years. The gap has a defined beginning and a roughly defined end. The return is planned if not precisely scheduled.

At the middle of the spectrum: one to three years. More open-ended. The intention is broader — not just to pause but to explore. What does the slow travel life actually feel like? What does the identity without the title actually reveal? What is the thing I want to build, and how long does it take to build it? The return is less defined. The gap-taker may come back with a completely different vision of what the next chapter looks like than the one they left with.

At the longer end: the gap becomes the life. Five years in, four continents, nineteen countries, no plans to stop. The gap did not pause the life. The gap became the life. The three paths of the book's final section — Return, Reinvent, Extend — are all valid, and the Extend path is the one where the gap never formally ends because it was never intended to. It was always the permanent restructured life.

My wife and I are building toward the longer end of the spectrum. Not necessarily the full nomadic version — we have things we are making that require infrastructure sometimes. But the permanent restructured life. Not two months in Australia and then back to what we left. A life that is genuinely different from the one the career organized — more intentional, more ours, more oriented toward what we are building together in the time we have.

We met later in life than most, and the time we have together is not infinite. That is not fear. It is the triangle made personal — and it is part of why the permanent restructured life matters more to us than the traditional retirement model ever could.

The permanent restructured life is not a retreat from ambition. It is ambition pointed in a different direction.

The Four Phases

Every Golden Gap — regardless of its length, its location, or the type of person taking it — moves through four internal phases.

They do not always arrive in a clean sequence. They overlap, repeat, compress, and expand depending on the person and the circumstances. But they are present in every gap in some form, and naming them gives the gap-taker a map for the territory they are crossing.

Phase One — Decompression. The gap begins before it feels like the gap. The first weeks are characterized not by freedom but by the strange, slightly disorienting experience of not being required. The inbox is not filling. The phone is not demanding. The calendar is empty in a way it has not been since childhood. The nervous system is recalibrating. The body is releasing pressure that has been present so long it feels like the baseline. This phase can feel like failure. It often feels like purposelessness or the specific anxiety of unstructured time. It is neither of those things. It is the decompression chamber that every deep-sea diver passes through on the way back to the surface. The pressure is equalizing. The phase typically runs four to eight weeks, sometimes longer for people who have been running very fast for a very long time. The instruction for Phase One is simple and frequently ignored: let it happen. Do not fill the silence with productivity. Do not judge the gap by the first month. The gap you planned for starts in Phase Two.

Phase Two — Exploration. The decompression lifts. The curiosity box opens. The world outside the apartment becomes interesting rather than effortful. The gap-taker begins to move — literally and figuratively — through the possibilities of the life they are designing. This is the phase of slow travel in its most active form. New cities. New rhythms. The templed-out wall arrives and is recovered from. The phase in which the gap-taker figures out their travel style — how long to stay, how fast to move, what kind of environment sustains them and what kind depletes them. Exploration is also internal. The gap-taker is discovering who they are without the title. What they reach for when the schedule is theirs. What makes them forget to eat lunch and what makes them watch the clock.

Phase Three — Design. The exploration yields data. The gap-taker knows their travel style. They know which types of environments sustain them. They know what they are curious about and what they are building and roughly how long it will take. Design is the phase in which the next chapter takes shape. The consulting practice gets its first clients. The book gets its first chapters. The partnership between the gap-taker and their partner finds its new rhythm. The permanent restructured life — whatever form it takes for this particular person — begins to have contours. Design is also where the financial architecture clarifies. The gap-sized portfolio is doing its work. The income threads are beginning to generate — slowly, unevenly, not yet at career levels, but real. The Maker is making. The thing is being made.

Phase Four — Decision. Every gap ends or transforms. The Decision phase is when the gap-taker chooses what comes next from the three paths available: Return, Reinvent, or Extend. Return: go back to something resembling the career, but on new terms with new clarity. Reinvent: the next chapter looks nothing like the career. The Maker launches. The consultant establishes. The creative builds. Extend: the gap becomes the life. The permanent restructured version. The Decision phase does not require a dramatic announcement. Most gap-takers find that the decision makes itself — that by the time they are in Phase Three, the direction is clear enough that Phase Four is simply the confirmation of what was already known.

The Gap You Are Building

A gap is not the same as a break. A break restores you to the previous state. A gap changes the state itself.

What you are building — whether it runs for six months or five years, whether it involves three continents or one quiet city where the work gets done, whether it ends in Return or Reinvent or Extend — is a deliberately designed period of your life in which you reclaim what the career consumed, reset the operating system that the career installed, and reposition everything you have built toward the life you are actually choosing.

The subtitle of this book promises three things.

Reclaim. Reset. Reposition.

The Golden Gap is where you do all three.

Not sequentially. Not neatly. Not without difficulty or uncertainty or the occasional week in Phase One where you wonder if you made a terrible mistake.

But fully. Deliberately. On your own terms.

That is what a gap actually is.

THE NUMBERS

Chapters 6 - 7

The financial architecture

CHAPTER SIX

The Cash Snapshot Living Lean and Eating Well

Here is the honest version of the financial conversation.

We did not have enough to retire. We had enough to go.

That distinction matters more than any spreadsheet. Retirement is a permanent exit from earned income, a bet that what you have accumulated will outlast you. The Golden Gap is something more specific and more limited: a runway. A calculated period during which the portfolio funds the life while the next thing gets built, explored, or decided. Not forever. Long enough.

When we looked at the actual cash — not the theoretical retirement number, but the real runway we had built through years of living deliberately tight — the stress did not disappear. But it reduced. Measurably. The number was not impressive by retirement-planning standards. By gap-funding standards, it was workable. And workable, when you have been running on empty for thirty-five years, feels like permission.

The concern was not whether we could afford to travel. We had already established that slow travel costs less than suburban American life — that is the next chapter. The concern was simpler and more practical: could we actually live the life? Could we cook from scratch in a foreign kitchen, shop at a local market with no car and limited language, and genuinely thrive — not endure — on a tight daily budget?

The answer surprised us.

Not because it was easy. Because it was better.

—

The Convenience Premium — What You Are Already Spending

Before the numbers of the Golden Gap make sense, you need to understand the number you are currently spending that does not appear clearly on any budget.

Call it the Convenience Premium.

It is not a single line item. It accumulates in the gaps between the categories — in all the small transactions that are not buying goods or services but buying back the time that the career consumed. Walk through a typical week in suburban American life and it is everywhere.

The grocery delivery fee because driving to the store on a weekday is impossible. The lawn service because weekends are for recovery, not yard work. The dry cleaning pickup because who has time to drop it off. The car wash subscription because the car needs to be presentable and there is no Saturday morning free to wash it yourself. The meal kit subscription that delivers three times a week because cooking from scratch requires planning you cannot do at 7pm after a full day. The Tuesday restaurant because nobody had the energy to cook and the Tuesday restaurant has become the silent agreement the household makes about the state of its exhaustion.

The task rabbit for the thing that needed doing. The Amazon Prime impulse purchase that would have cost half as much if you had had twenty minutes to think about whether you needed it. The Uber because parking was a nightmare and your phone said surge pricing but what was the alternative. The storage unit for the things you do not have time to sort through.

Each one of these transactions is rational in the context of a life that has no time. Together they add up to something significant. A suburban American couple can easily spend $12,000 to $17,000 per year on the Convenience Premium — money that evaporates not into experiences or assets or memories but into the recovery from a life organized around a career that consumed everything.

During the Golden Gap, the Convenience Premium disappears.

Not through discipline. Not through a budget spreadsheet or a deprivation mindset. It disappears because the life structure that generated it is gone. When you have time, you do not need to buy it back. The lawn service becomes irrelevant because there is no lawn. The dry cleaning becomes irrelevant because the wardrobe shifts. The Tuesday restaurant becomes irrelevant because Tuesday morning you went to the market and bought something interesting and you have been thinking about what to make with it ever since.

This is not sacrifice. This is the natural outcome of removing the thing that made those transactions necessary.

The Market, the Scan, and the Recipe

There is a specific rhythm to the food life of the Golden Gap that takes about two weeks to find and then becomes the best part of the day.

It starts at the market.

Not the supermarket — the local market. In Lisbon it is the Mercado de Campo de Ourique or the Mercado da Ribeira. In Chiang Mai it is the JingJai Farmer's Market. In Medellín it is the Mercado de Paloquemao. Every city worth slow traveling has one — a covered or open-air market where the produce is seasonal and local and the vendors know what came in this morning.

The prices at a local market in Lisbon will stop you the first time you see them. A kilogram of chicken fillets runs approximately €7. Oranges are €1.70 per kilogram. Tomatoes are around €2.30 per kilogram. A bottle of quality Portuguese wine costs €5. Fresh bread is €1.50 a loaf.

Fresh produce at local markets is often 15% to 30% cheaper than large supermarkets, especially for seasonal vegetables.

You are not shopping for the week in a single car-trunk load. You are shopping for today, and maybe tomorrow. Small basket. Walk home. This is how most of the world buys food and it produces better meals than the American system of bulk purchasing and refrigerator archaeology.

Before you put anything in the basket, you scan it.

The Yuka app is free, available in English, and works anywhere in the world on any product with a barcode. Point the camera at any packaged product and it scores the ingredient quality on a simple scale — green means good, orange means questionable, red means put it back. Once you start using Yuka you cannot unknowingly buy something that is quietly terrible. The highly processed product gets a red score and stays on the shelf. The simpler alternative costs less and scores green.

What you discover scanning your way through a Portuguese supermarket for the first time is that the baseline quality of ordinary food is higher than what most American packaging conceals. A jar of pasta sauce in Lisbon contains tomatoes, olive oil, and basil. Its American equivalent contains high fructose corn syrup, modified starch, and natural flavors. The local product is not the expensive organic option — it is just the regular product. The food culture is different and the ingredient honesty is built in.

Then you get home with the basket and you open Claude or ChatGPT.

You type something like: I have chicken thighs, flour, butter, olive oil, eggs, carrots, garlic, and a can of peas. We are two people. What should I make for dinner?

Here is exactly what comes back.

—

Garlic Butter Chicken with Glazed Carrots and Peas

Season two chicken thighs with salt and pepper and dredge lightly in flour. Sear in a mix of olive oil and butter over medium-high heat for five minutes per side until golden. Remove the chicken, add sliced carrots and whole garlic cloves to the same pan, cook two minutes, then return the chicken and add a splash of water. Cover and simmer fifteen minutes until cooked through. In the last two minutes, stir in the drained peas and a knob of butter to glaze everything together. Serve straight from the pan.

—

Estimated cost of those ingredients at Lisbon market prices: chicken thighs approximately €3.50, carrots €0.60, garlic €0.30, butter €0.50. Total for two: approximately €5 to €6. Roughly $5.50 to $6.50 USD.

The equivalent at a mid-range Lisbon restaurant — a chicken dish, vegetables, shared starter, two glasses of local wine: approximately €35 to €45 for two people.

You just saved €30, cooked something better than what the restaurant would have produced, spent forty-five minutes doing something genuinely satisfying in a kitchen in a foreign city, and ate a meal that Yuka would score green from the first ingredient to the last.

This is not a cooking story. This is a financial story. Multiply that €30 saving by twenty-five dinners a month and you have saved €750 — approximately $820 — in a single month from one meal change alone. The kitchen is not a nice amenity in the monthly apartment. It is the financial engine of the whole model.

The Kitchen Dividend

The bonusnachos.com couple — the five-year, four-continent, nineteen-country documented case study that grounds this book's financial argument — spent $554 per month on food for two people across their best-documented European year. That includes all groceries and all meals out.

For context: the average American household spends approximately $475 per month on food away from home alone — not counting groceries. Eric and Katie were spending less in total, across Europe, including both cooking and eating out, than the average American was spending on restaurants only.

The mechanism is the kitchen. A furnished apartment with a real kitchen changes the food economics completely. You cook most meals. You eat out for the experience — a local lunch, a special dinner, the neighborhood place that the market vendor recommended — rather than eating out as the default because cooking requires time you do not have.

A couple eating every meal out at modest Lisbon prices spends approximately $60 to $80 per day on food. At $70 per day that is $2,100 per month. Eric and Katie spent $554 per month. The kitchen dividend — the difference between cooking most meals and eating out most meals — is approximately $1,500 per month. That is $18,000 per year. More than half the entire bonusnachos annual budget, recovered by the simple act of having a kitchen and using it.

This is why every chapter of this book that discusses accommodation emphasizes the kitchen as a non-negotiable. Not for lifestyle reasons. For financial ones.

What Thriving Tight Actually Looks Like

Living lean during the Golden Gap is not austerity. It is redirection.

The money that was going to the Convenience Premium now goes nowhere — the Premium has dissolved. The money that was going to meals out now goes to groceries and one or two genuinely chosen restaurant experiences per week. The money that was going to the car — gas, insurance, maintenance, parking, depreciation — now goes nowhere because you are in a walkable city and the transport card costs €40 a month.

What you have is not less. What you have is differently organized.

You have time to cook, so you cook well. The Yuka scan means you are putting better ingredients in your body than you were buying in the suburban supermarket rush. The AI recipe assist means the cooking is interesting rather than repetitive — a different dish every night from whatever the market had this morning. The result, consistent with what the gap-takers who have documented their experience report, is that you feel better. Not just psychologically. Physically.

The body that was running on takeout and convenience food and the chronic low-grade inflammation of a highly processed diet starts to change when the diet does. The walking — built into every walkable base camp city, automatic rather than scheduled — adds up. The sleep improves when the inbox stops filling at 6am. The markers that were quietly moving in the wrong direction quietly begin moving back.

You are not trying harder. You are living differently.

The Home Exchange — Your Biggest Cost, Solved Creatively

Accommodation is the largest single line item in any gap budget. The bonusnachos data shows it at 46% of total spend — approximately $1,197 per month in Europe for a furnished apartment with a kitchen in a walkable neighborhood.

That is not an unreasonable number. It is less than many Americans spend on their mortgage or rent at home. But it is the number to manage most actively because it is the one with the most creative solution space.

The base model is the monthly rental. Airbnb, Furnished Finder, and local listing sites all offer monthly rates that run 40% to 50% cheaper than nightly rates. A furnished one-bedroom apartment in Lisbon that costs $150 per night on a weekend trip books for $1,800 to $2,400 per month — the equivalent of $60 to $80 per night. The kitchen is included. The neighborhood is real. This is how the $1,197 monthly figure is achieved.

But there is a more creative model that can reduce accommodation cost dramatically or eliminate it entirely.

Home exchange.

The mechanism is simple. You list your home on a platform. Other members list theirs. You arrange to stay in their home — sometimes simultaneously, sometimes sequentially through a points system — while they stay in yours or someone else's. The annual membership costs $100 to $220. The accommodation costs nothing beyond that.

Three platforms dominate this space.

HomeExchange is the largest, with over 360,000 homes in 155 countries. It operates on a GuestPoints system that eliminates the need for simultaneous exchanges — you earn points by hosting guests at your home and spend points to stay at other members' homes, anywhere in the network, on your own schedule. Annual membership is $220. Members report saving thousands of dollars annually. The GuestPoints token model works especially well for gap-takers who are traveling full-time and cannot host simultaneous exchanges.

People Like Us is a fast-growing platform with members and listings in over 100 countries, offering four exchange types including simultaneous, non-simultaneous, and points-based options. The community has an unusually warm social dimension — active Facebook groups where members share local knowledge and genuine hospitality. This is the kind of community where you might find your first readers.

Kindred takes a curated approach. Every member is vetted, all listings are primary residences rather than investment properties, and the system charges per night rather than an annual fee. More expensive per stay but higher quality control.

What home exchange provides beyond the financial saving is the specific experience of living where someone actually lives. A real home in a real neighborhood, with a real kitchen stocked the way a real person stocks a kitchen — and sometimes a note from the host about the best coffee shop on the corner, the market that opens on Thursday mornings, the restaurant that tourists have not found yet.

That note is worth more than the accommodation it accompanies.

The Points Runway — Starting Now

The first year of flights and hotels in the Golden Gap does not have to be paid in cash. It can be paid in points accumulated through normal household spending in the years before departure.

This is not a complicated strategy. It requires starting two to three years before departure, choosing the right two or three credit cards, and putting your normal household spending — groceries, dining, utilities, travel — on those cards instead of a debit card or a card with no rewards. Nothing changes about what you spend. The points accumulate quietly on the same purchases you are already making.

The foundation for most Golden Gap readers is a three-card stack.

Chase Sapphire Preferred or Reserve is the starting point. Part of the Chase Ultimate Rewards system, points transfer at a 1:1 ratio to ten airlines and four hotel chains including Air France/KLM, British Airways, United, and World of Hyatt. The Preferred costs $95 per year. The Reserve costs $550 but includes a $300 annual travel credit. The sign-up bonus — typically 60,000 to 75,000 points — is worth $1,200 to $1,500 in travel when redeemed through transfer partners. Apply for this card first.

American Express Gold earns 4x points on groceries and 4x on dining. For a household spending $800 to $1,200 per month on food, this card accumulates points faster than almost any other option available. American Express Membership Rewards transfer to seventeen airline programs. The card costs $325 per year but the grocery earning rate makes it the strongest day-to-day accumulation engine in the portfolio.

A flat-rate backup for everything else. Capital One Venture X earns at least 2x on all purchases, costs $395 per year, and includes a $300 annual travel credit. Use this card for any purchase that does not earn bonus points on the Sapphire or the Gold.

The power of this stack over two to three years of normal household spending is significant. Sign-up bonuses alone — applied for in sequence, six to twelve months apart — can generate 175,000 to 250,000 points across all three programs. Ongoing accumulation at blended bonus rates adds another 100,000 to 150,000 points over two years of household spending.

At transfer partner redemption values, 350,000 combined points represents $7,000 to $10,000 in business class flights and hotel nights. For a couple, that is the first two months of the gap — flights, accommodation, ground transport — funded entirely by points accumulated from grocery runs, restaurant dinners, and electricity bills.

One rule worth printing and keeping somewhere visible: transfer points to an airline only when you have confirmed award availability for a specific flight. Once transferred, points stay in that airline's program. They cannot come back. Research the award first. Confirm the seat exists. Then transfer.

Living Lean Is Not Living Small

The life that the Golden Gap buys — the market, the kitchen, the Yuka scan, the AI recipe, the home exchange, the points-funded flights — is not a reduced version of the life you are leaving.

It is a differently organized version. One in which the things that were quietly consuming your health, your time, and your sense of presence have been removed. One in which the $12,000 to $17,000 you were spending on the Convenience Premium is no longer leaving your account. One in which the food is better, the sleep is deeper, the mornings belong to you, and the kitchen on a Tuesday is a pleasure rather than a problem.

You are not living smaller.

You are living intentionally.

The numbers that demonstrate how this is financially possible — the portfolio math, the withdrawal rates, the regional cost comparisons, the portfolio scenarios for three different types of gap-takers — are in the next chapter.

They are worth reading.

CHAPTER SEVEN

The Numbers

Let me say something honest before the data arrives.

Numbers are not everyone's thing.

If you are the person who skips to the back of the instruction manual, who hands the tax documents to someone else, who has a good general sense of your financial situation but finds the mechanics of portfolio withdrawal rates and Roth conversion ladders genuinely uninteresting — this chapter is still worth reading. Not all of it. The regional cost snapshots in the middle are practical and specific and do not require any financial knowledge to use. The portfolio scenarios near the end will tell you clearly which financial profile you have and what the math looks like for your specific situation.

But if the Roth conversion section makes your eyes cross, you have permission to skim it. Bookmark it. Come back to it with your financial advisor. The plain-English summary at the end of this chapter puts the entire picture in four points.

What this chapter does not do is let you skip the numbers entirely.

Because here is the honest truth about the Golden Gap: it is a financial decision. The philosophy is real, the psychology is real, the case for taking it is compelling — but the case has to be funded. You cannot Reclaim, Reset, and Reposition your life after fifty if the portfolio runs out in year two. The numbers matter. They are more favorable than most people assume, but they are still numbers, and pretending they do not exist would make this book inspirational and useless.

So. The numbers.

—

A Warning About Numbers

Before the data lands, three things worth knowing.

First: all cost figures in this chapter are real and documented but they are snapshots. Costs change. Exchange rates fluctuate. A city that was affordable in 2024 may be more expensive by the time you arrive if the slow travel community discovers it and rent prices follow. Use the regional figures as starting points for your own research, not as fixed budgets.

Second: the bonusnachos.com figures — $28,050 per year for two people, five years documented — are the most trustworthy data set in this chapter because they are the most specific, the most transparent, and the longest running. They are also one couple's numbers in one set of circumstances. Your numbers will differ based on your health needs, accommodation approach, travel style, home situation, and how much wine you drink. Use the bonusnachos data as the benchmark and adjust from there.

Third: the portfolio math here assumes you are drawing down the portfolio without earned income. Many Golden Gap readers — especially the Maker type — will generate some income during the gap. Every dollar of earned income reduces the portfolio draw by a dollar and extends the runway. The math gets better as income develops. The figures here represent the floor, not the ceiling.

The $28,050 — What It Actually Includes

Let me unpack what five years of documented slow travel life actually costs, category by category.

Eric and Katie at bonusnachos.com spent an average of $28,050 per year across four continents and nineteen countries. Their best-documented European year broke down as follows.

Housing and Accommodation — 46% / $12,882 per year / $1,074 per month

Fully furnished apartments with kitchens, leased monthly rather than nightly. Not hostels. Not budget guesthouses. Real apartments in walkable neighborhoods in major European cities — Lisbon, Budapest, Seville, and others. Monthly lease rates applied at a 40% to 50% discount from nightly rates. Utilities and WiFi included in most cases. The figure includes occasional shorter stays between longer base camps but the base camp model kept this number manageable.

Food — 21% / $5,880 per year / $490 per month

For two people. Covers all groceries and all meals out. The kitchen in the monthly apartment is the financial engine — most meals are cooked at home from market ingredients, with eating out reserved for two to three times per week. Quality is not compromised. Quantity is managed through cooking rather than ordering. The $490 monthly figure includes coffee, wine, occasional restaurant dinners, and the entire grocery shop.

Health and Insurance — 11% / $3,086 per year / $257 per month

Includes their international high-deductible catastrophic coverage policy at $1,092 per year for the couple — approximately $91 per month — plus all out-of-pocket medical costs. The Budapest broken wrist is included in this figure: five visits, four x-rays, three casts, total cost $831. The figure also includes over-the-counter medications and dental work done in lower-cost countries. This is not premium comprehensive international health coverage — it is a high-deductible policy covering catastrophic events, not routine care.

Transport — 3% / $840 per year / $70 per month

The number that stops people when they see it. Three percent. $70 per month. For context, the total European year transport figure was approximately $85 — zero flights, primarily local transit passes, occasional trains between base camps. The base camp model is the reason. When you are living in a city for a month, you do not need to fly anywhere. You take the metro. You walk. The €40 monthly Lisbon transit pass covers unlimited bus and metro travel. The occasional train to a nearby region costs €15 to €25 round trip.

Everything Else — 19% / $5,330 per year / $444 per month

Entertainment, activities, cultural experiences, clothing, personal care, household items for the apartment, technology, subscriptions, visa fees, banking fees, and miscellaneous. This is where personal spending style has the most impact. Eric and Katie are not monks — they see museums, attend local events, and live a genuinely full life. The number is what it is because the base camp model eliminates the tourist trap spending that characterizes vacation travel.

Total: $28,050 per year. $2,338 per month. $77 per day for two people.

The worst year — including the broken wrist and a market correction — cost

$31,100. Even at the worst year, the annualized daily cost for two was $85.

—

The Regional Snapshots

The bonusnachos figures are European. The Golden Gap reader has choices. What follows is a comfortable but not extravagant slow travel life at the base camp model — monthly apartment with kitchen, mix of cooking and eating out, public transport, and a modest activities budget — across the primary regions. Each region gets a prose description and a monthly snapshot table. Read both or just the table, depending on how you think.

Western Europe — Portugal, Spain, France

Western Europe is the default first base camp for most English-speaking Golden Gap readers and for good reason. The infrastructure is excellent. Healthcare is world-class. The food culture is extraordinary. English proficiency is high in Portugal and adequate in most major Spanish and French cities. The monthly rental market is well-developed.

Portugal is the standout value within Western Europe. Lisbon in particular has become the slow travel world's most talked-about base camp — a walkable, beautiful, historically rich city with extraordinary food and wine at prices significantly below other Western European capitals. A couple can live comfortably in Portugal on $2,500 to $3,000 per month. Porto and smaller cities run meaningfully lower. Lisbon runs toward the higher end of that range as monthly rental prices have risen with the city's global popularity.

The honest caveat: Lisbon accommodation prices have risen significantly in the past three years. Monthly rates in desirable walkable neighborhoods now run €1,200 to €1,800 for a furnished one-bedroom. Budget accordingly or choose Porto, Coimbra, or the Alentejo region for significantly lower accommodation costs with similar food quality and lifestyle.

Porto and smaller Portuguese cities run approximately 20–30% lower across all categories.

Eastern Europe — Hungary, Georgia, Serbia, Albania

Eastern Europe is the value proposition that Western Europe offered ten years ago. Hungary, Georgia, Serbia, and Albania are non-Schengen — meaning they do not count against your 90-day Schengen allowance — and they are dramatically cheaper than their Western counterparts while offering high quality of life, exceptional food, and increasingly sophisticated infrastructure.

Georgia has become the fastest-growing slow travel destination in the region. Most nationalities receive a full year visa-free. Tbilisi has extraordinary food, world-class wine, breathtaking mountain scenery within easy reach, reliable fast internet, and a monthly rental market that has developed rapidly. Budapest remains one of the most underrated base camp cities in Europe — grand architecture, exceptional thermal baths, a vibrant food and coffee culture, and costs 30% to 40% lower than Lisbon or Madrid. Albania on the Adriatic coast offers Mediterranean beaches at a fraction of Greek or Italian prices.

The honest caveat: the language barrier in Georgia and Serbia is real. English proficiency is lower than in Portugal or

Spain. Research your specific city carefully and lean on the local expat community for orientation.

Tbilisi runs approximately 20–30% cheaper than Budapest across all categories. Albania (Tirana, coastal towns) is comparable to Tbilisi.

Southeast Asia — Thailand, Vietnam, Malaysia

Southeast Asia offers the strongest value proposition in the world for slow travelers with Western income. Chiang Mai in northern Thailand is the canonical base camp — a large, sophisticated city with an enormous expat and nomad community, excellent internet, world-class Thai food at street-stall prices, and monthly rental options ranging from budget studios to luxury condos with pools and gyms. The city is 80% cheaper than New York by most cost-of-living measures.

A couple in Chiang Mai living comfortably — nice accommodation, frequent dining out, hiring a cleaner, weekly massages — spends under $2,000 per month with nothing held back.

One significant caveat that belongs in any honest discussion of Chiang Mai: the air quality takes a serious hit during the burning season from February to April, and the heat can be oppressive between May and June. Golden Gap readers spending extended time in Chiang Mai should plan to relocate during the February to April window — Southern Thailand, Bali, Vietnam, and Malaysia all serve as excellent seasonal alternatives.

Vietnam (Da Nang, Hoi An, Hanoi) and Malaysia (Penang, Kuala Lumpur) offer similar value with different cultural experiences and visa structures. Vietnam in particular has become a preferred alternative for travelers seeking Chiang Mai's affordability with better year-round air quality.

Da Nang, Vietnam and Penang, Malaysia are comparable to Chiang Mai in overall cost. Bali, Indonesia runs slightly higher in accommodation during peak season.

Latin America — Colombia, Mexico, Panama

Latin America's primary advantage for North American slow travelers is time zone alignment. The Maker who needs to maintain communication with US clients, the consultant taking occasional calls, the content creator whose audience is primarily American — all benefit from a time zone that keeps working hours synchronized.

Medellín has become one of the world's most popular slow travel destinations. The city's transformation over the past two decades is one of the great urban stories of the twenty-first century. Eternal spring climate averaging 72 degrees year-round, sophisticated infrastructure, extraordinary coffee culture, and a cost of living that has risen with its popularity but remains dramatically lower than North American equivalents. A comfortable lifestyle for a couple in Medellín ranges from $1,500 to $2,000 per month.

Mexico offers proximity — easy access to the United States for family visits, widely accepted US payment systems, and no language barrier in major expat destinations like San Miguel de Allende, Oaxaca, and Puerto Vallarta. Panama provides the best-structured retiree visa in the region through the Pensionado program.

The honest caveat: safety research is essential for any Latin American destination. Medellín has transformed but specific neighborhoods require research. San Miguel de Allende, Oaxaca, and the Yucatan region of Mexico have established expat communities with well-understood safety dynamics. Do the research before booking, not after.

Mexico City, San Miguel de Allende, and Puerto Vallarta run 10–30% higher than Medellín. Panama City is comparable to Medellín.

—

Where the Average 53-Year-Old American Actually Stands

Here is the number that makes this chapter real.

The median retirement savings for Americans aged 45 to 54 is $115,000, according to the Federal Reserve Survey of Consumer Finances. The median for those aged 55 to 64 is $185,000 — far below the $1.26 million that Americans believe they need to retire comfortably.

Read that again. The median. The middle number. Half of Americans in their mid-fifties have less than $185,000 saved for retirement.

The conventional retirement conversation looks at that number and sees a crisis. The gap between $185,000 and $1.26 million is insurmountable for most people following the standard script.

The Golden Gap conversation looks at that number differently.

$185,000 at a 4% withdrawal rate generates $7,400 per year. That is not enough to fund a gap independently. But paired with a home that can be rented or exchanged, some part-time consulting or content income, and the cost reduction that geographic arbitrage provides in Southeast Asia or Latin America — the math begins to move.

More importantly: $185,000 is the median. Half the readers of this book have more than that. Significantly more, in many cases. Americans in their fifties have an average retirement savings balance of $1,020,838 and a median of $438,866. The average is pulled upward by high-net-worth individuals, but $438,866 is still a workable number for the right kind of gap.

The conventional retirement number is built around a $60,000 to $80,000 per year

American suburban lifestyle. The gap-sized number is built around $20,000 to $30,000 per year of intentional slow travel. Those are different calculations with dramatically different outcomes.

Three Portfolio Scenarios

Which one is yours?

The Comfortable — $600,000 to $900,000

At $600,000 and a 3.5% withdrawal rate, the portfolio generates $21,000 per year — enough to fund a Chiang Mai or Medellín slow travel life with room to spare. At $900,000 and a 4% withdrawal rate, the portfolio generates $36,000 per year — enough for comfortable European slow travel at bonusnachos levels with $8,000 to $10,000 remaining for flexibility.

At this portfolio level, the math is favorable. The question for The Comfortable is not whether they can afford the gap but whether they will give themselves permission to take it. The retirement planning conversation has been telling them for years that the number is not big enough. But that conversation was calculating against an $80,000 per year suburban American lifestyle, not a $28,000 per year slow travel life.

The withdrawal rate under the gap's spending level drops below 3.5% at the lower end of this range and approaches 3% at the upper end. At a 3.5% withdrawal rate over 30 years with a stock-weighted portfolio, research consistently shows the portfolio ending larger than it started. The portfolio is not depleting. It is growing.

The Runway Runner — $300,000 to $600,000

At $300,000 and a 4% withdrawal rate, the portfolio generates $12,000 per year — not enough to fund the gap independently but enough to contribute materially when combined with other elements. At $600,000 and 4%, $24,000 per year — approaching the gap-sized number for Southeast Asia or Latin America.

The Runway Runner needs geographic arbitrage to work. Southeast Asia or Latin America rather than Western Europe as the primary base camp. The home exchange model where possible. And — critically — some income generation during the gap. Not a full salary. Not immediate. But the consulting engagement that starts at month four, the content that begins generating modest income at month eight, the book that finds its first readers at month twelve.

Research consistently shows that meaningful supplemental income from a new venture requires six to twelve months of sustained effort to develop. The Runway Runner starts building before that income arrives and sustains the portfolio until it does. This is the Maker profile executed under financial pressure — which, historically, is where the most focused work gets done.

The Just Enough — $150,000 to $300,000

At this portfolio level, the gap requires the full toolkit deployed simultaneously. A home rented or exchanged to generate accommodation credits and offset holding costs at home. Southeast Asia or Latin America as the primary base camp where costs under $1,500 per month for two people are achievable. Part-time consulting or freelance income beginning as early as month two, drawing on career expertise that took decades to build.

The math at this level is tight but workable if the elements align. $200,000 at a 4% drawdown generates $8,000 per year from the portfolio. A consulting engagement at $50 to $100 per hour for ten hours per week generates $26,000 to $52,000 per year — immediately closing the gap between portfolio income and living costs and potentially generating savings.

The Just Enough scenario is not the comfortable version of the Golden Gap. It is the committed version. The reader who takes it is betting on themselves — on the market for their expertise, the viability of their direction, the discipline of the budget. That bet is not guaranteed. But it has been made successfully by thousands of people who had exactly this financial profile and chose the gap anyway.

The gap does not require wealth. It requires enough and a plan.

—

The Tax Architecture

This section covers the Roth conversion ladder and the ACA health insurance strategy in specific terms. If the plain-English summary at the end of this chapter is more your speed, skip there now. If you want the mechanics, they follow.

The Roth Conversion Ladder

Most people in their fifties have the majority of retirement savings in traditional 401(k) or IRA accounts — pre-tax money that will be taxed as ordinary income when withdrawn. In retirement, when Social Security income and required minimum distributions stack on top of portfolio withdrawals, the effective tax rate on those withdrawals can be substantial.

The gap creates a specific window to address this permanently.

During the gap, earned income is zero or near zero. The standard deduction for a married couple filing jointly is approximately $30,000. This means the first $30,000 of income you generate — including Roth conversions from traditional accounts — is federally tax-free. The 12% bracket covers the next $89,000 of income.

Combining these two thresholds, a gap couple can convert approximately $119,000 from traditional to Roth accounts per year at a blended federal tax rate under 10%. Done over a three-year gap, this moves $350,000 or more into permanently tax-free Roth accounts at a total tax cost of approximately $30,000 to

$35,000 — an effective rate under 10% on money that would otherwise be taxed at 22% to 24% or higher in traditional retirement.

The five-year Roth rule: converted funds must sit in the Roth account for five years before being withdrawn tax-free. Plan the conversion timing accordingly relative to when you expect to need those funds.

Work with a fee-only advisor. The XY Planning Network at xyplanningnetwork.com specializes in exactly this type of planning for pre-retirement transitions. Fee-only means they do not earn commissions — they charge a flat fee or hourly rate and their advice is not influenced by what they are selling. This conversation is worth having at least twelve months before departure.

The ACA Strategy

The Affordable Care Act's premium tax credit system is tied to Modified Adjusted Gross Income. In the gap years, when earned income is low and Roth conversions are managed to keep reportable income below 400% of the federal poverty level, a couple may qualify for substantial subsidies on ACA health insurance during any US-resident periods.

The 2024 federal poverty level for a two-person household was $20,440. At 400% — $81,760 — a couple qualifies for some subsidy. At lower income levels the subsidy is more substantial. The precise calculation depends on your state, the year's premium rates, and the income you report including Roth conversions.

The practical outcome: the same low-income years that make the Roth conversion ladder valuable also create an opportunity to access ACA health coverage at reduced or zero premium cost during periods spent in the United States. Two apparent financial vulnerabilities — no employer health insurance and low income — become strategic advantages when structured correctly.

The South Dakota Option

The bonusnachos couple maintained South Dakota as their legal domicile throughout their five gap years. South Dakota has no state income tax. For a couple executing Roth conversions at the federal level, eliminating state income tax on those conversions saves an additional 3% to 10%

depending on which state they would otherwise owe.

Establishing legal domicile in South Dakota requires a physical presence visit, a South Dakota mailing address (virtual mailbox services work for this purpose), and a South Dakota driver's license. It is a legitimate, widely used strategy among long-term slow travelers. Consult with a tax professional familiar with nomadic taxation before implementing. These three strategies together — the Roth conversion ladder, the ACA subsidy optimization, and domicile selection — are the gap's tax architecture. All three require a fee-only advisor. None are optional if you are serious about making the math work as well as the life does.

—

The Plain-English Summary

Four points. The entire financial picture in plain English.

One — The gap costs approximately $28,000 per year for two people at the bonusnachos documented level in Europe. Southeast Asia and Latin America cost $17,000 to $28,000 per year. Western

Europe costs $28,000 to $39,000. These are real figures from documented real-world experience, not estimates.

Two — The gap-sized portfolio number is dramatically lower than the retirement number. At $28,000 per year and a 3.5% withdrawal rate, you need $800,000. At $20,000 per year in Southeast Asia, you need $570,000. Many readers of this book are closer to these numbers than the retirement planning conversation has suggested.

Three — The gap years are the best years to execute Roth conversions. Zero earned income plus the standard deduction creates a window to move significant money from traditional to Roth accounts at federal tax rates under 10%. Talk to a fee-only advisor at xyplanningnetwork.com before departure. This conversation is worth having.

Four — The median 53-year-old American has $115,000 to $185,000 saved. The gap math does not work at this level without geographic arbitrage, some income generation, and the full accommodation toolkit. But it works. The

Just Enough scenario is harder than The Comfortable scenario. It is not impossible.

THE LIVED EXPERIENCE

Chapters 8 – 13

The psychological and relational journey

CHAPTER EIGHT

The Four Stages of the Gap

Nobody tells you about the cliff.

They talk about the freedom. The adventure. The clean slate. The version of yourself that emerges on the other side of the career. That is all real. But they skip the part where you are standing at the edge looking down, having committed to the leap, and you do not know how deep the water is or whether it is cold.

That is what the first days felt like.

My job was gone. Two or three days of absorbing that. Of feeling the hit of the thing that had organized my professional identity for decades being removed without my permission. But here is what I noticed almost immediately: after two or three days, I was not thinking about what had ended. I was thinking about the runway. What the possibilities were. How to extend what I had so that the next chapter had enough time to build properly.

It felt good. Not triumphant — it was too uncertain for that. But right. Like a hard decision that turned out to be the correct decision even though you had not made it yourself.

And then I slept.

Not until noon. I woke at 8:30 and I was rested. Properly, fully, physiologically rested in a way that had not been available to me in years. Not the sleep of exhaustion that sends you unconscious and delivers you back to Monday depleted. The sleep of a nervous system that is finally not running the threat-detection protocol in the background all night.

That was the first signal that something had fundamentally changed.

The cliff had not ended me. The water was there. And it was not cold.

—

A Map for the Territory

Every Golden Gap moves through four stages.

Not in a perfectly linear sequence — they overlap, reverse, compress, and expand depending on the person and the circumstances. A difficult week in Stage Two can drop you back into the disorientation of Stage One. A direction that turns out to be wrong can send Stage Three back to Stage Two for recalibration. The map is not the territory.

But having the map is still better than navigating without it.

The four stages correspond to identifiable psychological and physiological processes that research consistently documents in people who leave high-stress careers — the decompression arc, the curiosity recovery, the identity redesign, and the decision that forms when the other three have done their work.

They also correspond to the three words in this book's subtitle.

Reclaim happens in Stage One. The body and mind recovering what the career consumed — sleep, cognitive clarity, the specific peace of a day that asks nothing of you.

Reset spans Stages One through Three. The operating system upgrade from anxiety as fuel to curiosity as fuel. This does not happen at a single moment. It is a process that the stages create the conditions for.

Reposition happens in Stage Three. The skills, the experience, the accumulated capability of thirty-five years pointed at the life you are designing rather than the organization you were serving.

Stage Four is the confirmation. The decision that emerges from the other three.

Stage One — Decompression

Reclaiming What the Career Consumed — Typical duration: weeks one through eight, sometimes longer

The gap begins before it feels like the gap.

The first days are characterized not by freedom but by the specific strangeness of not being required. The inbox is not filling. The calendar has nothing in it. The pressure that had been present so long it felt like the baseline of existence is no longer there.

This should feel like relief.

For most people, it does not. Not immediately.

What it feels like initially is disorientation. A slightly unmoored quality, the way you feel on the first morning of a week's vacation before your body has registered that the week has actually started. Except this is not a week. And the nervous system does not know how to process the absence of something it has been organizing itself around for thirty-five years.

The science behind this is unambiguous and important.

Chronic burnout does not merely leave you feeling exhausted. It leaves a physical signature in the brain. MRI-based research found that people suffering from burnout showed more pronounced thinning in the prefrontal cortex — the brain's primary cognitive control center — compared with healthy controls. Burnout patients showed larger amygdalae and shrinking in the caudate, both correlating with perceptions of workplace stress. Beyond anatomical changes, research shows burnout disrupts creativity, problem solving, and working memory. Even individuals who appeared to perform normally on cognitive tests were found to be recruiting significantly more neurological resources to achieve those results — working harder just to maintain average performance.

The brain that arrives at the threshold of the Golden Gap is not the same brain that started the career. It has been changed — measurably, physically — by the sustained load of chronic professional stress. Decompression is not a psychological metaphor. It is a literal physiological process of neural repair and hormonal recalibration.

The Sleep Signal

The first indication that Stage One is working — usually within the first week — is sleep.

Research shows that after just two to three days of removing work stress, people average an hour more of good quality sleep and experience an 80% improvement in reaction times. That is two to three days. Not weeks.

The mechanism is cortisol. Chronic occupational stress keeps cortisol elevated — the stress hormone that suppresses melatonin production and keeps the threat-detection system running overnight. When the stressor is removed, cortisol begins to normalize. The sleep that follows is different in quality from the sleep of exhaustion. It is restorative rather than merely unconscious.

I noticed this within the first week. Not sleeping until noon — waking at 8:30, rested. That specific quality of waking that is different from the waking of a person who has slept enough hours but whose nervous system was working all night. The body sending an early signal that the recalibration had begun.

The Critical Distinction: Vacation vs. Gap

Here is the research finding that matters most for understanding why Stage One requires the full gap and cannot be accomplished on two weeks' leave.

Vacation does alleviate perceived job stress and burnout, and a respite from work does diminish strain levels. However, declines in burnout immediately after vacation return to pre-vacation levels within four weeks of resuming work.

Four weeks. The vacation effect lasts four weeks.

The gap effect is structural rather than temporary. The difference is not the length of time away from the office — it is whether the stressor itself has been removed or merely interrupted. The nervous system that knows it is going back in two weeks never fully releases the load. The vacation is a brief suspension of the pressure. The gap is the actual removal of the thing that was generating the pressure.

People who change jobs, reduce hours, or take extended leave often recover two to three times faster than those who try to push through. The nervous system cannot heal while the threat remains active.

The gap removes the threat. The vacation merely pauses it.

What Accelerates Stage One

Six things reliably shorten Stage One. And the remarkable insight — the one that makes the slow travel model look specifically designed for decompression rather than merely incidentally beneficial — is that the slow travel life provides five of the six automatically, through structure rather than discipline.

Sleep is the foundation. Seven to nine hours nightly, consistent timing. The gap provides this automatically because the inbox stops at 6am and the calendar is empty.

Movement is the second most reliable accelerator. Physical activity, even a 20-minute walk, reduces stress hormones and boosts mood. Research shows 5,000 steps per day is enough to help keep depression at bay. The base camp model in a walkable city provides this automatically. You walk to the market. You walk to the coffee shop. The steps accumulate without scheduling.

Social connection reduces the physiological stress load measurably. The slow travel life provides ongoing low-stakes social contact that the suburban commuter life often does not — the market vendor who recognizes you, the neighbor in the building, the language class, the home exchange host who left recommendations.

Nature exposure calms the nervous system through well-documented mechanisms. The walkable base camp city almost always provides this — the waterfront, the park, the hills, the coastal path. It is built into the geography.

Removal of the stressor is not merely one accelerator among many. It is the primary accelerator, often making recovery two to three times faster than attempts to recover while still under stress. The gap delivers this completely and structurally.

The deliberate practice — the one thing the slow travel life does not provide automatically — is a simple journaling habit. Ten minutes in the morning. Not a therapeutic practice. Not a formal protocol. Just the act of writing what is present. What you notice, what you are thinking, what surprised you yesterday, what you are curious about. Journaling processes the emotional residue of the career years and clears cognitive space for what comes next.

A related deliberate practice worth naming: the internal critic that says 'I should be doing something productive' at 9am on a Tuesday is not a report on what is actually required of you right now. It is the career's operating system still running after the career has ended. You do not have to believe it. You can notice it, recognize it as old programming, and let it run without letting it organize your day. That simple act of noticing rather than obeying is the core of what cognitive behavioral therapy calls reframing — and it

is one of the most powerful things you can
do in Stage One.

What Stage One Looks Like in Practice

The first week is strange. The second week
is stranger in a different way — the
strangeness of something that was acute
becoming something that is settled. By
week three the sleep is consistently better.
By week four the mornings have a different
quality — not purposeless, but genuinely
open in a way that feels earned rather than
forced.

The body is doing most of the work. Your
job in Stage One is not to accelerate the
process through productivity. It is to allow
it. Walk. Sleep. Eat well. Write ten minutes
in the morning. Do not judge the gap by
the first month.

The gap you planned for starts in Stage
Two.

Stage Two — Exploration

*Resetting the Operating System — Typical
duration: months two through six*

Something lifts.

It is not dramatic. It does not announce itself. But at some point in the second month — sometimes earlier, sometimes later — the quality of the mornings changes again. The strange disorientation of Stage One gives way to something that feels like curiosity. The world outside the apartment becomes interesting rather than effortful. The calendar that was oppressively empty starts to feel like possibility.

The curiosity box opens.

For me, this happened faster than the typical timeline suggests — because my curiosity box had been cracking open before my job ended. I had known the position was tenuous. I had been quietly allowing myself to wonder what came next. Within a week of the exit, I was deep in learning artificial intelligence tools, not because I had planned to but because something that had been suppressed for years was suddenly running free. The specific relief of intellectual curiosity given permission to go where it wants rather than where the job requires.

Within a few weeks I had a detailed outline for the first book.

That outline was not the beginning of Stage Three — it was the confirmation that Stage Two was fully operational. The curiosity box was not just open. It was running at full power for the first time in years.

What Stage Two Actually Is

Stage Two is the reset. The operating system upgrade from anxiety as fuel to curiosity as fuel.

For most of the career years, the primary motivational fuel was anxiety. Not crippling anxiety — functional anxiety. The specific forward pressure that comes from having responsibilities, metrics, performance reviews, organizational expectations, and the implicit knowledge that the career requires continuous performance to be maintained. Anxiety as fuel works. It produces results. It is also exhausting in a way that only becomes fully visible when it stops.

Curiosity as fuel is different. It produces different results in different directions at a different pace. It does not require an external threat to activate. It requires permission and space — the specific conditions that the gap creates.

Brain imaging research shows that the default mode network — a system linked to creativity and problem solving — activates when you are not focused on urgent tasks. Extended breaks and travel create the conditions for this network to run freely, producing the insights and creative connections that the always-on work brain suppresses. The career suppressed the default mode network for thirty-five years by keeping the urgent-task system continuously activated. Stage Two is what happens when the urgent-task system finally gets a rest.

The External Exploration

Stage Two is also where the slow travel life becomes most actively rewarding.

This is the phase of new cities, new rhythms, new markets, new coffee shops, new coastal paths. The phase where the base camp model shows its specific genius — the four-week minimum that allows the gap-taker to move from tourist to quasi-resident, to know which bakery opens earliest and which path to the waterfront avoids the morning crowds.

The diminishing marginal utility of novelty — the templed-out wall discussed in

Chapter 14 — is managed in Stage Two by depth rather than speed. The gap-taker in Stage Two is not chasing novelty. They are inhabiting a place long enough to discover what is actually interesting about it rather than what is photographable about it.

The download conversation begins in Stage Two. The separate outings that give the couple something genuinely new to tell each other at dinner. The specific pleasure of having something to say that the other person did not witness and did not know was coming.

The Internal Exploration

Alongside the external exploration, Stage Two is where the gap-taker begins to discover who they are without the title.

What do you reach for when the schedule is yours? What makes you forget to eat lunch? What time do you naturally wake when there is no alarm and nothing required? What subject has been in the back of your mind for fifteen years that you finally have the unstructured time to actually pursue?

The curiosity that Stage Two releases is data. It is information about the design work that Stage Three will do. The gap-taker who pays attention in Stage Two arrives at Stage Three knowing their direction rather than having to guess at it.

My direction became clear within weeks. The books in my head — the ideas that had been compressed by the career into occasional late-night notes and fleeting intentions — suddenly had a container and a calendar and the specific permission that comes from having paid for a professional AI subscription — and actually filling those hours every single day rather than letting the access sit largely unused as it had during the career.

That subscription was the moment Stage Two became real. Not the travel to the other side of the world. The tool. The daily commitment to the work that the curiosity had identified.

Stage Three — Design

Repositioning Everything — Typical duration: months four through twelve or beyond

The exploration yields data. The gap-taker knows their travel style. They know which environments sustain them and which deplete them. They know what they are curious about and what that curiosity wants to build.

Stage Three is where the next chapter takes shape.

Not as a vague intention — as a direction with contours. The Maker starts making at the level of sustained, daily, real work rather than occasional motivated bursts. The consultant identifies the market for their expertise and begins the outreach that produces the first client. The writer finishes the first draft and discovers, somewhere in the editing, that they can actually do this. The couple figures out what the permanent restructured life actually looks like rather than what they imagined it would look like when they were planning it from the suburban driveway.

Stage Three is the Reposition. Everything the career built — the competence, the self-knowledge, the network, the hard-won judgment of someone who has been tested at length — pointed at the life you are designing rather than the organization you were serving.

The Design Work

The design work of Stage Three is both practical and identity-level.

At the practical level: the consulting practice finds its first client. The manuscript reaches its first complete draft. The home exchange network produces its first significant accommodation saving. The Roth conversion ladder is executed for the first tax year. The monthly budget is refined from theoretical to actual as real spending data accumulates.

At the identity level: the answer to the party question — what do you do? — is being built rather than inherited. Stage Three is where the gap-taker stops answering that question with what they used to do and begins answering it with what they are doing.

This shift is not instantaneous. It happens through accumulation. The first chapter that makes you smile when you read it. The first client call that feels like genuine peer collaboration. The first morning when the day's work is the most interesting problem in front of you rather than something you are doing in service of someone else's priorities.

When Stage Three Stalls

Stage Three stalls when the direction chosen in Stage Two turns out to be wrong.

This happens. The direction that looked clear from the vantage point of early exploration reveals itself, in the sustained daily work of Stage Three, to be less interesting than expected. The consulting market that seemed robust is not quite shaped the way the gap-taker assumed. The book that was vivid as an idea is more difficult to build than imagined.

The right response is not crisis. It is redesign.

Return briefly to Stage Two. Ask the curiosity questions again. What did Stage Three reveal about what is actually interesting versus what was theoretically attractive? What did the work of daily execution teach about the direction? What would you do differently with what you now know?

Stage Three stalls are not failures. They are the gap doing what the gap is designed to do — revealing, through direct experience, what the career years never had the space to reveal.

Stage Three and the Couple

For the Couple at a Crossroads, Stage Three is when the joint design work becomes most specific and sometimes most difficult.

The individual direction of each partner has been clarified by Stages One and Two. Stage Three requires those individual directions to be integrated into a shared design. What does the permanent restructured life look like when both people's Stage Two data is on the table simultaneously?

This requires genuine conversation rather than assumed alignment. The couple who talked about the shared life in Stages One and Two — in the abstract, in the aspirational — needs to have more specific conversations in Stage Three. About income. About geography. About what makes each partner's work feel meaningful. About what the next chapter requires that the current design provides or does not provide.

These are not easy conversations. They are the most important conversations the gap enables.

Stage Four — Decision

The Three Paths Forward — Arrives when it arrives

Every gap ends or transforms. The Decision is not a single moment — it is the recognition of a direction that the other three stages have been quietly building.

Most gap-takers find that by the time they are consciously considering Stage Four, the decision has already been made. The direction is clear. The choice is not what to do next but whether to acknowledge what has already become obvious.

Three paths forward.

Return — going back to something resembling the career, but on new terms with new clarity. Not the same role, the same organization, the same operating system. A version of professional engagement informed by what the gap revealed — about what is worth doing, what the body can sustain, what the work needs to feel like to be worth the cost. Many people who take the gap with the intention of returning find that they return to something significantly different from what they left, having used the gap to redesign the terms of engagement rather than exit the category entirely.

Reinvent — the next chapter looks nothing like the career. The Maker has launched something. The consultant has a practice. The writer has a manuscript. The creative business is generating income that is not yet at career levels but is moving. The identity that the gap revealed gets fully inhabited rather than kept as a side project. This is the path that requires the most patience — the patience to keep making before the making pays, to trust the direction before the market confirms it.

Extend — the gap becomes the life. Not a pause before the next thing. The thing itself. The slow travel life that was supposed to be temporary reveals itself, somewhere in Stage Three, as the permanent restructured life that this book's subtitle describes. The gap-taker who extends is not avoiding the decision. They are making it — choosing the gap not as an interlude but as the ongoing structure within which the next chapter will be written, whatever that chapter turns out to be.

The Decision Makes Itself

I did not make my Stage Four decision on a specific day. It made itself across the weeks and months as the work accumulated, as the books in my head became chapters on a screen, as the curiosity that had been locked in the career's box ran free and revealed what it had always been waiting to build.

The gap did not give me a plan. It gave me the conditions under which a plan became visible.

That is what Stage Four produces. Not a clean decision handed down from some elevated moment of clarity. The gradual emergence of a direction that the gap has been quietly preparing all along.

The leap off the cliff.

The water was there. It was not cold.

It was the beginning.

CHAPTER NINE

Who Are You Without the Title?

Two weeks ago someone asked me what I did for work.

I hesitated.

Not because I did not know the answer. Because the honest answer did not have a clean label yet. The version I had used for decades — the industry, the role, the company, the title — no longer applied. I had spent years in the foodservice business, running operations, fixing problems, flying in when something needed to be solved and moving on when it was. I had led teams I was proud of. I had managed accounts and locations and relationships across the country. I had been, in every professional sense, someone with a clear answer to that question.

And standing there, two weeks ago, I did not have one.

So I said what was true. I told him I used to work in foodservice. That now I was a consultant and a writer. That I was building something.

It probably sounded awkward to him.

It was the most honest thing I had said about myself in years.

—

That moment — the hesitation, the search for words, the slight awkwardness of an answer that does not fit neatly into a single noun — is not a failure. It is a threshold.

It is the moment when the identity the career built starts to loosen, and the identity you actually are starts to become visible underneath.

Most people never reach this moment deliberately. They either hold onto the career identity until it is taken from them, or they are Spat-Out and find themselves on the other side of it without a map. The transition is involuntary and therefore disorienting. They did not choose to stop being the person the job title described. The choice was made for them.

The Golden Gap makes the transition intentional.

It says: before the career identity is stripped away by circumstance, you are going to choose to set it down yourself.

Carefully. With both hands. And then you are going to find out what is underneath.

That is the work of this chapter.

The Identity the Career Built

Here is something worth naming honestly.

The career did not just give you income. It gave you a self.

It told you what to do with your Monday morning. It gave you a title that answered the party question without effort. It surrounded you with colleagues who knew your competence and your history. It organized your days into a structure that carried you forward without requiring you to consciously choose your own direction every morning.

For thirty or forty years, the career was the container of your identity. Not the whole of it — you were also a parent, a partner, a friend, a person with interests and opinions and a particular way of moving through the world. But the career was the container that held everything else together. The thing that, when someone asked who you were, gave you the first and easiest answer.

Take the container away and the contents do not disappear.

But they do need to find a new shape.

The INSEAD Warning

The research on identity transition after career exit is not reassuring if you go into it unprepared.

An INSEAD Business School study of people who had achieved financial freedom — who had, by any external measure, succeeded in building the life they wanted — found something unexpected. Many of them were lost.

They grappled with feelings of emptiness and anxiety. They struggled when asked the simple question — what do you do now? They cycled through answers that did not satisfy. I am an investor. I am a full-time parent. I do nothing. None of them felt true. None of them felt like enough.

The researchers found that the biggest challenge was not financial. It was not logistical. It was the question of identity and purpose — deciding, out of seemingly boundless possibility, who to be and what to build next.

The FIRE community documented the same failure mode independently. People who spent years fixating on a financial number — a portfolio target, a date, a threshold — arrived at that number and discovered that the spreadsheet had not prepared them for the psychological reality of life on the other side. The money problem was solved. The meaning problem had never been addressed.

This is not a character flaw. It is a design flaw.

The career was so good at providing identity that most people never had to build one consciously. It was automatic. It came with the job. And so when the job ends — whether by choice, by circumstance, or by the deliberate design of the Golden Gap — the identity question arrives fully formed and completely unanswered.

Who are you without the title?

The Curiosity Box

Let me tell you about the thing that surprised me most.

When I had a true day off during the working years — a real one, not a day where the phone was technically silent but the inbox was loading in the background — I slept until noon. Not because I was lazy. Because my brain and body were exhausted. The sustained cognitive load of the career, the travel, the constant problem-solving, the management of teams and relationships and crises — it was consuming energy I did not know I was spending. The day off was not leisure. It was recovery.

Now I wake up at around eight-thirty.

I eat breakfast. I watch the morning show. I turn off the television around nine-thirty, open my laptop, check my emails, and start researching. Not because I have to. Because I want to. Because the thing I am building is interesting to me, and the day ahead is mine, and the curiosity that drove me for decades has finally found something to drive that is purely and entirely mine.

I have been spending time in online communities lately — Reddit communities,

mostly, where people are figuring out
variations of the same thing I am figuring
out. And I keep seeing it — the moment
someone describes discovering that their
curiosity is back. That they are interested
in things again. That they woke up at six in
the morning because they had an idea and
wanted to chase it.

I think of this as the curiosity box opening.

You had this box when you were young.
Before the career, before the mortgage,
before the performance review and the
quarterly target and the stakeholder
management. You had a natural curiosity
about the world — about ideas, about how
things worked, about what was possible.
You chased things for the pleasure of the
chase. You learned things for the pleasure
of learning.

The career did not destroy that curiosity. It
just put it in a box, locked it, and put the
box somewhere high up on a shelf where
you could not reach it from your desk.

The Golden Gap gets you a ladder.

When the structure that consumed your
energy is removed, when the stress that
was burning your cognitive fuel is gone,

when the schedule that filled every available hour with someone else's priorities is finally empty — the box opens. Not all at once. Not dramatically. But gradually, over the first weeks and months of the Golden Gap, you will find yourself interested in things again. Genuinely interested. Not because you have to be. Because you are.

The curiosity that drove you through thirty years of problem-solving and team-building and innovation — that curiosity did not retire. It was waiting.

The Sydney Hills

My wife and I have been climbing hills.

Sydney has hills the way a foreign language has false friends — they look manageable from a distance and then reveal themselves to be something else entirely up close. There are staircases that connect neighborhoods, harbor walks that turn into genuine climbs, streets that angle upward at a gradient that makes you reassess your cardiovascular assumptions.

I am climbing them.

Not because I set a fitness goal or downloaded a wellness app or made a resolution. Because we live here right now, and the hills are between us and the things we want to see, and walking is how you inhabit a place rather than visit it.

My body is doing better than it was.

Not dramatically, not in the way that makes for a compelling before-and-after photograph. But measurably. Sustainably. In the way that comes from consistent movement through interesting terrain rather than the start-and-stop guilt cycle of a gym membership you visit three times in January and then feel bad about in March.

This is one of the things nobody tells you about the Golden Gap. The physical change is not the result of discipline. It is the result of design. When you live in a walkable place and your days are unscheduled and the world outside your door is interesting, you move. Naturally, consistently, and without the exhausting self-negotiation that exercise requires when you are tired and stressed and already depleted from a day of someone else's priorities.

The career was not just consuming your time and your identity.

It was consuming your body.

The Golden Gap gives it back.

Anxiety as Fuel

Here is the honest version of what the working years looked like, emotionally.

You were driven. You are still driven — that does not go away, and in fact the Golden Gap reader is typically someone whose drive was one of the things that made them successful. But during the career, for most people, that drive ran on a specific fuel.

Anxiety.

The anxiety of the unfinished project. The anxiety of the underperforming team member. The anxiety of the quarterly review, the stakeholder presentation, the flight delay that threatens the meeting, the email that arrived at eleven PM and probably needs a response. The anxiety of being responsible for things you do not fully control and accountable for outcomes you cannot fully guarantee.

None of this is dramatic. None of it looks like clinical anxiety from the outside. It is the low-level, chronic, professionally acceptable anxiety of someone who cares about their work and has a lot at stake. It is normal in the career context. It is expected. It is, in many high-performing corporate environments, the primary fuel of the engine.

The problem is what it does to the body and the mind over thirty-five years.

It wears the instrument down. Not catastrophically. Gradually. The way a road wears down under traffic — perfectly functional on any given day, visibly different after a decade of use.

And it shapes what you reach for. When anxiety is your fuel, you reach for the thing that quiets the anxiety. You solve the problem because the unsolved problem is uncomfortable. You clear the inbox because the full inbox is stressful. You take the meeting because declining feels risky. You run on the pressure of what needs to be escaped rather than the pull of what wants to be built.

The shift from anxiety as fuel to curiosity as fuel is not a small thing.

It is a different way of being in the world.

Curiosity as Fuel

I am surprised, honestly, at how unworried I am about money.

I probably should be more worried. I am building income streams rather than drawing a salary. I am creating rather than executing someone else's strategy. The financial floor is different than it was. The certainty is lower.

And yet.

The not-worried feeling is not naivety. It is not denial. It is something more interesting than either of those things.

It is the experience of working hard on something that is genuinely mine — writing, researching, building, learning — and finding that the work itself is sustaining in a way that work-for-someone-else was not. The energy comes from a different place. It replenishes differently. The hours I spend on this project do not deplete me the way the equivalent hours in a corporate context depleted me. They build something.

I believe the money will come. Not as a passive expectation. As a working hypothesis being tested by consistent daily effort. I keep learning and creating. Everything takes hard work and patience. I know both of those things in my bones from the career. I am applying them now to something that is mine.

This is what curiosity as fuel feels like.

It is not the absence of effort. It is effort that flows from interest rather than obligation. Work that pulls you toward it rather than pushing you from behind. The difference between running toward something you want and running away from something you fear — the speed may be the same but the experience is completely different, and over time the direction of travel matters more than the pace.

The anxious drive gets you through a career.

The curious drive builds a life.

There is a financial dimension to this shift that most people do not see coming.

During the career, time was scarce and money bought it back. Delivery fees, cleaning services, lawn care, restaurant markups — all of it was the rational price of a constrained life. You were not being lazy. You were trading money for the time you did not have.

The Golden Gap changes the constraint. Time is no longer scarce. The question flips from whether something is worth the time it saves to whether it is worth the money it costs. Same transaction. Opposite question. And the answer changes almost every time. The market visit is not an errand. It is the morning. The cooking is not a burden. It is the culture. The curiosity that opens during the gap reaches into the domestic and the practical as much as the adventurous and the exotic. You find yourself interested in figuring things out again — not because you have to, but because the curiosity box is open and everything is interesting now.

The Question Underneath the Question

When someone asks what you do, they are asking a practical question.

But there is a deeper question underneath it, and that is the one the Golden Gap is really answering.

Who are you?

Not what do you produce. Not what value do you generate for which organization. Not what title describes your position in which hierarchy. Who are you — as a person, with a particular history and a specific set of capabilities and a genuine curiosity about certain things and a genuine indifference to certain other things?

The career answered this question efficiently but superficially. It gave you a role and the role gave you an identity. It required very little self-knowledge to function, because the organization's needs provided the frame and your job was to fit inside it.

The Golden Gap requires self-knowledge.

Not the performed self-knowledge of the career development workshop or the leadership coaching session. The actual kind. The kind that comes from being alone with your own thoughts long enough to notice what they are. The kind that comes from having a genuinely unstructured day and noticing what you reach for. The kind that comes from being in a new place with no one's expectations to manage and no performance to maintain and discovering what you are actually like when none of that is required.

This is why the first phase of the Golden Gap — the Decompression phase — can feel disorienting even when everything is going well. You have been asking the career's questions for so long that your own questions feel unfamiliar. The silence where the job used to be is not comfortable at first. The absence of urgency feels like a problem to solve.

It is not a problem. It is a clearing.

And into that clearing, gradually and then more rapidly, the real questions come.

What do I actually care about? What have I been postponing? What did I stop reaching for because the career made it impractical? What am I curious about when no one is watching and nothing is at stake?

Those questions are the beginning of the identity that comes after the title.

You Are Not Starting Over

One of the fears that keeps people from taking the Golden Gap is the feeling that they will have to start from zero. That leaving the career means abandoning everything they built. That the skills, the knowledge, the relationships, the hard-won expertise of thirty years are suddenly worth nothing.

This is precisely backwards.

The person who takes the Golden Gap at fifty-five is not starting over. They are starting with everything.

They are starting with thirty years of understanding how organizations work and why they fail. With a network built across decades of professional relationships. With a specific set of skills that are genuinely rare because they were developed through sustained practice rather than theoretical study. With the self-knowledge that only comes from having been tested, under pressure, over a long period of time.

What the Golden Gap does is not erase this. It redirects it.

I was the person who flew in when something was broken and figured out how to fix it. I worked with everyone on the team. I moved problems from one state to another. I managed the complexity of operations and people and logistics across different locations, different cultures, different challenges.

That is not a career description that expires. It is a capability description that applies to almost any domain.

The consultant and writer I am becoming is not a different person from the operations manager I was. He is the same person, applying the same capabilities to a different set of problems — specifically, to problems he chose because he is curious about them rather than problems he was assigned because the organization needed them solved.

The title changes. The person does not.

What changes is the direction of the energy. From outward to inward. From executing someone else's strategy to building your own. From accumulating position to deploying it.

The thirty years of the career were not wasted. They were preparation.

For this.

The New Answer

I am still working on my answer to the party question.

Not because I do not know who I am. But because the honest answer is more interesting than the old one and takes slightly longer to say.

I am someone who spent decades solving operational problems for large organizations and discovered, when the structure was removed, that what I had been doing was less interesting than what the experience had prepared me to do. I am someone building independent income streams because I would rather work hard for myself than work hard for someone else's quarterly numbers. I am someone who woke up one day without a title and found, to my genuine surprise, that the person underneath the title was more interesting than the title had suggested.

I am a consultant and a writer. I am someone who climbs hills in Sydney with his wife on a Tuesday morning because that is what the Golden Gap makes possible. I am someone whose curiosity box is open, who is not stressed about money in the way that a person in my situation probably should be, who believes that the harder you work on something that is genuinely yours the more likely it is to become real.

That is a complicated answer to a simple question.

But the question was never really simple.

And the complicated answer is the true one.

Designing the Identity That Comes Next

The Golden Gap is not just a period of travel and exploration. It is a design laboratory for the identity that follows it.

Most people arrive at the end of a career and discover, too late, that they had been outsourcing the question of who they are to the organization that employed them. The organization provided the frame. The title, the role, the colleagues, the daily structure — all of it told you who you were without requiring you to figure it out yourself. And then it ended, and the frame was gone, and the question arrived for the first time with nowhere comfortable to land.

The Golden Gap encounters this question deliberately, in the middle of the career rather than at the end of it. It says: while you still have resources, while you still have health, while you still have the time and energy to do something with the answer — let's find out who you actually are.

Not through therapy or coaching or journaling prompts, although all of those have their place. Through experience. Through the discovery of what you reach for when the schedule is yours. Through the observation of what makes you forget to eat lunch and what makes you watch the clock. Through the specific, personal, irreplaceable education of being in the world on your own terms for long enough to know what your own terms actually are.

The Golden Gap does not give you a new identity. It reveals the one you already had.

And then it gives you the time, the resources, and the freedom to build your life around it.

Five Honest Reflections

One: The identity the career gave you was real and earned and worth honoring.

It is also not the whole of you. The Golden Gap is not a rejection of who you were. It is an expansion of who you are.

Two: The hesitation when someone asks what you do is not a failure. It is a threshold. The answer is getting more honest. Give it time.

Three: The curiosity box does not open all at once. In the first weeks of the Golden Gap, the silence where the structure used to be can feel like emptiness. It is not. It is space. They are different things.

Four: You are not starting over. You are starting with everything. The thirty years of the career were not a detour from the life you actually wanted. They were the preparation for it.

Five: Anxiety as fuel gets you through a career. Curiosity as fuel builds a life. The transition between the two is the work of the Golden Gap. It is the most important work you will do.

CHAPTER TEN

The Relationship Reset

There was a notification buzzing in my pocket.

Not one specific notification — the general condition of a life organized around immediate response. The phone that never fully went to sleep because the job never fully went to sleep. The email that arrived at 11pm and would still be there at 6am demanding an answer. The low-grade background hum of professional obligation that followed me from the office to the hotel room to the dinner table to the couch where I was supposedly present with my wife.

I was there. I was also not there.

The career consumed not just time but the specific emotional resource that a relationship requires to actually function — presence. The ability to be fully in the room. To hold someone's hand without part of your nervous system monitoring the inbox. To listen to a story without processing a problem from three hours ago in the background. Presence is not a feeling. It is a physiological state. And chronic professional stress makes it physiologically difficult to achieve.

When the job ended, the notifications stopped.

And something happened that I had not anticipated. I had patience again. Not performed patience — the effort to appear calm while something else runs underneath. Actual patience. The specific quality of attention that comes from a nervous system that is not managing seventeen competing demands simultaneously. I could sit with her. Talk to her. Hold her without the buzzing. Be in the room in the way that the career had been quietly preventing for years.

She loved that I was home. That she could call out to me. That I would answer without the distracted half-presence of someone who is technically available but operationally elsewhere. She could walk by and say hello and the hello would land rather than bounce off the invisible wall of professional preoccupation.

This is not a romantic story. It is a physiological one. The career had been spending down a resource that the relationship needed. The gap stopped the spending. What returned was not something new — it was something that had always been there, finally visible again.

That is the Relationship Reset.

—

What the Career Was Doing to the Partnership

Before the reset, there was the slow erosion.

It does not announce itself. The couple who has been together for twenty years does not sit down one day and decide to stop being fully present to each other. The erosion happens incrementally, in the accumulation of nights when one or both partners came home too depleted to give what the relationship needs. In the meals where the phone was on the table. In the conversations that were interrupted, abbreviated, or conducted in the half-present way of people who are technically available but operationally elsewhere.

The research on this is consistent and sobering. Studies examining couples over four years found significant crossover effects — partners of individuals with higher workloads experienced greater declines in marital satisfaction over time. Higher partner workloads prove consistently detrimental to relationship functioning. Work-related stress reduces the quality of marital interactions because individuals under chronic stress are less emotionally available to their partners.

Less emotionally available. That phrase is doing a lot of work.

Think about what that looked like in practice. The partner who came home from a day of meetings and travel and managing metrics and being always on — and arrived at dinner with nothing left. Not nothing for this conversation specifically. Nothing. The specific nothing of someone who has been talking and performing and managing and responding all day and arrives at the one relationship that should be the most important one with the tank empty.

The relationship was not the problem. The career was the drain.

I spent days talking to people. By the time I returned to a hotel room or flew home, the last thing I wanted was more conversation. I wanted silence. Mindless television. A meal that required no negotiation. Rest for the bones that had walked ten miles and the mind that had been running the enterprise software gauntlet. This is not a character flaw. It is the predictable physiological outcome of a demanding career that consumed everything and left the residue for the relationship to absorb.

The residue. That is what the relationship was running on. Whatever was left after the career had taken what it needed.

The gap stops the drain.

The Amplifier Effect — The Honest Part

Here is the piece of research that the chapter needs to name directly, because the reader who is already in a strained relationship needs to know it before the gap begins.

Research consistently shows that extended leave and the post-career transition reinforce the quality of marital relationships rather than change them. The effect is positive in already happy marriages. In unhappy, conflict-ridden marriages, the effect is adverse.

The gap is not a relationship repair tool. It is an amplifier.

What is already good gets better — sometimes dramatically better — when the stress drain is removed and the time and presence that the relationship has been running without are suddenly available. The partnership that was genuinely solid underneath the career's demands gets to rediscover what solid feels like when it is not being taxed daily.

What is already strained gets more visible. The career was providing structure and separation that managed the strain — the parallel tracks of employment giving each partner enough distance that the friction did not constantly surface. When that structure disappears and two people are suddenly together for most of the day with no buffer and no agenda and no organizational framework to hide inside, what was being managed becomes unavoidable.

This is not a diagnosis. It is information.

If you are reading this chapter and something in that paragraph landed with an uncomfortable recognition — if the prospect of extended unstructured time together produces something other than anticipation — that recognition is not a reason to skip the gap. It is a reason to have a conversation before the gap begins. About what you are each hoping the gap produces. About what the relationship needs that the career years have not provided. About whether the gap is something you are taking together or whether one of you is taking it and the other is along for the ride.

The reader who is fifty-plus has already survived enough of life to know when a relationship is genuinely fine and when it is managed. The gap reveals the difference. That revelation, handled honestly, is one of the most useful things the gap can do — even when it is not the most comfortable.

Research finds that the marital relationship is one of the most important resources for successful adjustment to the post-career phase. Couples who approach this transition with shared expectations and genuine communication adjust better than those who assume alignment they have not confirmed.

Have the conversation. The gap will have it for you eventually. Having it first is better.

What the Reset Actually Looks Like

For the couple whose relationship is fundamentally sound — and that is most of the couples who will read this book — the Relationship Reset is one of the most unexpected gifts of the gap.

Not because anything was wrong. Because the career had been spending down the resource of presence for so long that the relationship had learned to function without it. The couple that runs on efficiency — the abbreviated dinner conversation, the scheduled weekend connection, the intimacy that gets fitted into the margins — does not know what it is missing until the margins disappear and the whole canvas becomes available.

The canvas becoming available is initially disorienting. The couple that has been running on parallel tracks — separate careers, separate commutes, separate exhaustions meeting briefly at the dinner table — suddenly has nowhere to go but toward each other. That is not always immediately comfortable even in strong relationships.

The first adjustment is simply the presence itself. My wife loved that I was home. That she could call out. That I would answer. That simple thing — answering — had been complicated by the career for years. The answer was always partial, divided, running two processes simultaneously. The gap made the answer whole.

Then something else happened. Patience returned. The specific emotional availability that the career had been consuming — the capacity to be genuinely interested in another person's day when your own day has been entirely consuming — came back. Not as an effort. As a natural state. The stress drain had stopped. The resource was replenishing.

Complementary Skills and the Division of the Day

One of the things that makes the 24/7 togetherness of the gap sustainable — and for many couples genuinely wonderful — is the discovery that two people who have been running parallel lives have developed complementary rather than competing capabilities.

I have a poor sense of direction. My wife is not as observant as I am. In the suburban life organized around separate careers, these differences were irrelevant — each person was navigating their own domain. In the slow travel life organized around a shared adventure, they become assets. We are better at navigating the unfamiliar city together than either of us would be alone. The capabilities fit rather than duplicate.

This is not incidental. The gap creates the specific conditions for complementary strengths to become visible and valued in a way that the parallel-track career life does not. You discover what your partner is genuinely good at when you are depending on those capabilities in a real situation rather than in the abstract.

The other discovery — one that every couple who takes an extended gap reports in some version — is the value of shared quiet. Two people in the post-career phase may have different needs regarding silence versus conversation, reading versus planning, solitude versus engagement.

Recognizing this as a valuable balance rather than an issue of avoidance or rejection is important.

We do things in the house separately. We work on our projects in our respective corners. When we go out, we go out together — but the separate project time is not absence. It is the specific kind of privacy that makes togetherness feel chosen rather than obligatory. The couple that can be silent in the same room is a couple that does not need to perform connection. They are connected.

The separate outing is the practical implementation of this principle. Not every outing needs to be shared. I might go to a rugby match with her brothers. She might go to lunch with her mother. These are not separations — they are the mechanism that gives each person something to bring back. The download conversation at dinner works because each person went somewhere the other did not go and came back with something to tell.

This is the architecture of sustainable togetherness. Not constant proximity. Chosen proximity, structured by enough separation that the reunion is always a reunion rather than a continuation of the same unbroken stretch.

What the Gap Recovers

The research on couples who successfully navigate the post-career transition to extended shared time identifies a specific pattern. Partner support for self-expansion — actively encouraging each other's interests, new pursuits, and individual growth — predicts both relationship satisfaction and overall health one year into the transition.

This is not cheerleading. It is the specific act of being interested in what your partner is building, curious about what they are discovering, genuinely engaged with their individual direction rather than treating it as competition with or distraction from the shared life.

My wife is interested in what I am writing. I am interested in what she is pursuing. The gap created the time and the mental space for that interest to be genuine rather than performed — for the curiosity that the career years compressed into ten-minute end-of-day summaries to actually run at full length, in real time, with real follow-up.

We met twelve years ago. Later in life than most. We have things to explore together and not infinite time to explore them. That is not morbid — it is the specific urgency of people who found each other late enough to understand the value of what they found. The career was spending down time that belongs to the partnership. The gap is the reclamation.

Stress kills people and couples. That is not a metaphor. The research on chronic occupational stress and its effect on cardiovascular health, immune function, cognitive aging, and relational quality is unambiguous. The couple that removes the chronic stress from their shared life is not just doing something pleasant. They are doing something medically significant. They are extending the usable life of both the people and the partnership.

What the gap recovers is presence. Time. Patience. The specific emotional availability that the career had been spending down for decades. The version of each other that was always underneath the professional exhaustion — curious,

unhurried, capable of genuine attention —
becomes available again when the career
stops consuming the resources it was
running on.

We are stronger together now. More
patient. More secure. More honest with
each other in the specific way that comes
from having nowhere to hide and nothing
to perform. The career provided a
structure that made certain conversations
unnecessary because the days were too
short and the energy was too depleted to
have them. The gap makes them not just
possible but inevitable.

Inevitable is good. The conversations that
need to be had are better had by choice
than by crisis.

The Reset Is Not a Return

One clarification worth making before the
chapter closes.

The Relationship Reset is not a return to
how things were before the career. The
couple who has been together for twenty-
five years and takes the gap does not
emerge from it resembling the couple they

were at the beginning. They emerge as a more advanced version of the couple they became through all twenty-five years — with the career's drain removed and the gap's gifts added.

The patient attention that returns in Stage One of the gap is not the attention of two young people with nothing demanding it yet. It is the attention of two people who have built something together and are now, finally, building it for themselves rather than around someone else's organizational requirements.

That is a different thing. A better thing. Not innocent — experienced. Not uncertain — earned.

The gap does not give you back what the career took. It gives you what the career never allowed.

The reset is not to zero. It is to a version of the partnership that neither of you has fully experienced yet.

That is what is available on the other side of the decision.

CHAPTER ELEVEN

The Family Equation

My father had a stroke the week after we landed in Australia.

We had been in the country for about a week. Settling in, beginning to breathe differently, starting to feel the specific quality of a life that had stepped outside its previous structure. And then the phone call. My father was in hospital. Unresponsive for twenty-four hours. The doctors were watching. My mother was there.

My wife's father died of a stroke. She was younger than I am now when it happened. She was home from a trip, staying at her parents' house, and she was there. She knows what it means to be there and what it means to not be there. She looked at me when the news came and she understood the specific weight of the question before I asked it.

We talked. Are we going back?

The answer was no. Not unless he passed away. And if he passed away, we would go back not to attend to him but to help my mother cope with the loss, get things in order, make sure she could function. That was the calculation. Not cold — clear. My father would not want us on a plane in a panic. He would not want his health to interrupt our lives any more than mine interrupts his when he worries about me from his chair. That is how our family works. Low drama. Realistic. Each person trusted to manage their own situation and summoned only when the situation genuinely requires it.

He improved within twenty-four hours. He is still there.

But the week that followed was when I understood the Family Equation in its full complexity. The guilt arriving not as a slow simmer but as a specific moment — the news, the distance, the question of whether the right decision had been made. The answer was yes. It still felt like something.

This chapter is for the gap-taker who is working through that same equation.

—

The Guilt Is Real

Let us name it first, because dismissing it does not make it go away.

Middle-aged adults often face unique responsibilities that make it hard to step away from home. They may be caregivers for aging parents while also supporting adult children. This sandwich generation dynamic leads to feelings of guilt when taking personal time for travel — there is a concern that leaving loved ones, even temporarily, might seem selfish or neglectful, despite good intentions.

The gap-taker who is fifty-plus is frequently sitting at the intersection of two generations of obligation. Adult children who are launched but not fully independent. Aging parents who are managing but not invincible. The window between those two generations can feel like the least defensible moment to step away.

And yet it is precisely the moment when the gap is most valuable. Not in spite of the obligations but partly because of them. The person who takes the gap at fifty-five is taking it while their body can still carry the experience fully. The person who waits until everyone is settled, until the parents are stable, until the children are completely independent — that person is often waiting for conditions that never fully arrive.

The guilt is real. It is also frequently based on a misreading of the situation.

A geriatric social worker named Sofia Amirpoor puts it plainly: you must note that you are super special to your parents, but you are not that special that you are the absolute only one who can take care of them. There are other people who can provide the care that you do.

That is not a dismissal of the relationship. It is an accurate description of the support ecosystem that most aging parents have — or can build — that does not require the physical proximity of one specific adult child to function.

Every Family Is Different

The chapter that has to be written about this topic is not the one that tells you how your family should handle your gap. It is the one that helps you understand your family clearly enough to make the right decision for yours.

Some families are in each other's pockets by choice and by tradition. The Sunday dinner that has not been missed in forty years. The parent who calls every day and would experience any gap in the pattern as absence. The extended family system where proximity is structural — where your physical presence is genuinely woven into how the family functions.

Some families are not like that. Mine is not like that.

We live fifteen minutes from my parents. We see them a few times per month. We do not spend holidays together because they have close friends in their community. We take them to dinner — my father wears hearing aids, hates them, so crowds are a distraction. The dinner needs to be a conversation, not a performance. My mother drives well, for now. She has an enormous support system in the community where she lives — the kind of dense social fabric that seniors build over decades, where everyone knows who is in the hospital and for what and who just passed away. She is the glue. Strong, emotional, capable. She does not need me to be fifteen minutes away to be okay. She needs to know that when she needs me, I will come.

My children are grown and busy. A call once a week, if that. Their lives are full. So is mine. We are not in each other's pockets and nobody has suffered from the arrangement.

Understanding your family honestly — not the family you feel obligated to perform but the family that actually exists — is the first step in solving the Family Equation.

The Conversation Before You Leave

The guilt that is hardest to manage is the guilt that comes from conversations that were never had.

The gap-taker who leaves without a clear conversation with aging parents — about what the gap means, about what the communication plan looks like, about what circumstances would prompt a return — is carrying a weight that is not necessary to carry. The uncertainty is worse than the distance.

I spoke with my mother before we left. My father was asleep in his chair. She knew we needed to visit family — we were going to Australia to see her side of the family, people we had been away from for too long. She was good with me traveling. My father had traveled for work himself, in an era before cell phones, when distance was genuinely isolating. She managed then. She would manage now. Technology bridges all oceans in a way that simply was not possible when my parents were navigating the same separation.

That conversation was not dramatic. It was practical. We talked about what we were doing and why. We talked about what would bring us back — the specific circumstances rather than the vague anxiety. We did not perform the conversation. We had it.

The concern that leaving might seem selfish or neglectful is pervasive. Good intentions combined with clear communication transform the equation entirely. Most aging parents, confronted with an honest conversation from an adult child who is clearly not abandoning them but deliberately living, respond with more grace than the adult child anticipated. They raised someone who has the capacity and the courage to go somewhere. They know what that costs. Many of them wished they had done it themselves.

The conversation does not need to be long. It needs to be honest. What you are doing. How long you will be gone. What the communication rhythm will look like. What would bring you back. What you need them to understand about why this matters.

Technology Bridges All Oceans

This is not a platitude. It is a material fact that changes the Family Equation in ways that no previous generation of gap-takers had available to them.

My father traveled for work before cell phones existed. My mother's experience of his absence was genuine absence — no video call, no instant message, no photograph sent in real time. The distance was the distance and that was the entirety of what there was.

The gap-taker in 2025 is never more than a FaceTime call away from anyone they love. The video call that lets you see each other's faces, read each other's expressions, be genuinely present in real time from the other side of the world. WhatsApp messages that arrive instantly. Photographs shared the moment they are taken. The ability to be in the conversation of the family in a way that proximity used to be required for.

This does not eliminate the fact of distance. Certain things require physical presence — the emergency, the final weeks, the moments that matter in a bodily way. Those moments exist and the gap-taker needs to have thought through what they mean before departure.

But the daily fabric of family connection — the check-in, the story, the photograph of something funny or beautiful or worth sharing — that is fully available across any distance. The gap-taker in Australia is not cut off from their family in the same way that travel once required being cut off.

Plan the communication rhythm before you leave. Not a rigid schedule — a general shape. Weekly video calls. Daily messages when something comes up. The understanding that you are reachable, that you will respond, that the distance does not mean disconnection.

The family that understands the communication plan is the family that does not spend the gap imagining the worst.

The Pre-Gap Window With Aging Parents

There is a specific window — the months before the gap begins — that is also a specific window with aging parents. One worth treating deliberately rather than assuming will take care of itself.

This is the window when the parent is still the version of themselves you can have a real conversation with. When the hearing is still adequate, the memory is still reliable, the independence is still intact. The years ahead of aging parents are uncertain in ways that the years behind them are not. The gap-taker who leaves without using the pre-gap window for genuine connection is leaving something on the table that may not be recoverable in exactly the same form later.

Take them to dinner — the good dinner, not the convenient one. The dinner where the table is quiet enough for conversation rather than noise management. The dinner where there is time to talk about things that matter.

Ask the questions you have been meaning to ask. About their life before you. About the decisions they made and why. About what they wish they had done differently. About what they are proud of. These are the conversations that aging parents often want to have and rarely get invited into, because the adult children are too busy managing the practical dimensions of the relationship to create space for the human ones.

The pre-gap window with aging parents is the opportunity to make the family relationship something that can sustain a distance — because it is built on depth rather than proximity.

Schedule the family visits before you leave. Put them on the calendar as firmly as you put the first base camp. The visit home in month four. The video call on Sunday evenings. The trip home for the specific milestone that matters. Family as a destination — planned with the same intentionality as any other destination on the gap's itinerary.

The gap-taker who treats family visits as destinations arrives at them present and intentional rather than guilty and exhausted. The visit becomes a genuine visit rather than an obligation fulfilled.

What the Gap-Taker Models

There is a dimension of the Family Equation that almost nobody discusses — what the gap-taker is showing their family by taking the gap.

The adult children who watch their parent take the Golden Gap are watching a demonstration. Not of selfishness or irresponsibility or disregard for obligation. Of what is possible. Of what the second half of life can look like when it is designed rather than endured. Of what it means to take the window seriously rather than waiting for conditions that never arrive.

The most powerful thing any fifty-plus person can show their adult children is that the life after fifty is worth living on its own terms. That work does not have to be the organizing principle of an entire existence. That the curiosity and the adventure and the genuine presence in the world that the career compressed into margins can be reclaimed. That their parent, at fifty-five or sixty or sixty-five, is not winding down — they are doing something.

Every family has its own dynamic around this. Some adult children will worry. Some will be skeptical. Some will quietly envy and not admit it. Some will be inspired. What the gap-taker cannot control is the response. What they can control is the quality of the demonstration.

Go and do something worth demonstrating. Tell the story when you get there. Share the photographs. Bring the life back in a form that the people who love you can see and feel rather than just hear about in the abstract.

The aging parent who watches their adult child take the gap is also watching a demonstration. Of the life they raised someone capable of living. Of the values they passed on — the courage, the curiosity, the willingness to design rather than default. That is not a small thing to show the person who made you.

The Realistic Family Equation

Here is what the Family Equation actually adds up to for most gap-takers, worked through honestly.

The aging parents are almost certainly more capable of managing your absence than your anxiety about that absence suggests. They have support systems — communities, friends, neighbors, siblings, other adult children — that do not depend on your physical proximity to function. The genuine emergencies that would require your return are real but rare. Technology provides connection that proximity once monopolized. The conversation before you leave clarifies the plan and removes the uncertainty that generates the most guilt.

The adult children are adults. They are busy, they are living their lives, and the weekly call will sustain the relationship across any distance. What they need from you is not proximity — it is the knowledge that you are reachable, that you care, and that the relationship is genuinely important to you. The gap does not threaten that. The gap that is taken honestly, communicated clearly, and executed with genuine family contact along the way demonstrates it.

The guilt is real. It is also manageable. Not by dismissing it — by understanding what it is actually telling you. Most of the time it is not telling you that you should not go. It is telling you that the conversation has not been had yet. Have the conversation. The guilt reduces dramatically when the plan is clear and the family understands it.

Go. Check in regularly. Come home when it matters. Build the life that makes the story worth telling.

Your family is watching.

CHAPTER TWELVE

The External Skeptics and the Internal Skeptic

Nobody pushed back very hard.

That surprised me. I had anticipated more resistance — the concerned friend, the skeptical colleague, the family member who would need to be convinced. What I got instead was mostly curiosity. How long will you be gone? What will you do? And then, for most people, a kind of quiet that I eventually recognized as something other than disapproval.

It was envy.

Not the bitter kind. The honest kind. The recognition in someone else's face that what you are describing is something they have wanted and have not given themselves permission to want out loud. The person who says 'must be nice' is not always being dismissive. Sometimes they are being honest about a desire they have not yet figured out how to act on.

My older brother was not a skeptic about the gap. He had been a skeptic when I told him I had met an Australian woman, that we were engaged, that we were getting married. He learned, from that experience, that my decisions tend to be sound even when they look unusual from the outside. He has not been a skeptic since.

My grandmother — if she were still alive — would have been the loudest voice in the room. Not because she would have been unsupportive, but because she only knew one model. The traditional model. You work, you retire, you do not interrupt the sequence. Her concern would have come from love and from a framework that was complete and coherent within its own logic. It simply did not include this option.

The absence of significant external skepticism taught me something useful. The external skeptics, when they appear, are almost always asking the question from inside the traditional model. They are not wrong about the risks of deviating from the model. They are wrong about which risks matter most.

And the internal skeptic — the one running in my own head — is not asking about the decision at all. It is asking about the money. The impatience. The gap between where the income needs to be and where it currently is. That is a different kind of skeptic. More specific. More honest. And more useful to address.

—

The Work Devotion Norm

Before we get to the specific skeptics, there is a piece of social psychology worth naming — because it explains why the skeptics say what they say more accurately than any individual argument does.

One of the most common fears that prospective gap-takers express is their fear of what colleagues and employers will think. Social scientists call this the work devotion norm: the idea that work should take precedence over everything else in our lives, including family and health.

The work devotion norm is not a personal failing. It is a cultural framework that most working adults have absorbed so thoroughly that it feels like a fact rather than an assumption. The person who takes the gap is not just making a personal choice — they are implicitly questioning the norm. And people who have not questioned the norm themselves often respond to those who do with something that looks like concern but is actually discomfort.

The skeptic who says you cannot afford to leave your career is not wrong that careers take continuous investment to maintain. They are operating from the assumption that the career is the organizing principle of the life — that everything else is structured around the career's requirements. The Golden Gap is built on the opposite assumption. The life is the organizing principle. The career is a tool the life uses, not the other way around.

That is a genuinely different framework. Most skeptics are not arguing from evidence. They are arguing from the framework they have never examined.

The External Skeptics — By Type

The Career Skeptic

What they say: You cannot afford to step away. Your skills will atrophy. Your network will go cold. The gap in your resume will raise questions. You will not be able to get back in at the level you left.

What is actually true: For someone who is taking the gap as a permanent exit from the traditional career — which describes most Golden Gap readers — the career skeptic's argument is irrelevant. You are not trying to get back in at the level you left. You are building the next chapter on different terms.

For someone who might return to traditional employment after the gap — the Return path in Stage Four — the research answers the career skeptic directly. After taking an extended break, virtually all participants in research on the topic report renewed energy, creativity, and confidence. One nonprofit administrator described the shift plainly: I came back to work with fresh energy — from feeling like I was just a cog in the wheel to feeling like I had skills that were in demand, that people actually wanted to pay for.

The gap does not make you less employable. It makes you more interesting. The person with thirty-five years of career experience and a year of intentional design has a more compelling story than the person with thirty-six years of career experience. The story of what you did with the gap — the books written, the consulting clients found, the life deliberately designed — is not a liability. It is evidence of the kind of self-direction that organizations claim to want and rarely see.

The Financial Skeptic

What they say: You cannot afford to not be earning. Every year out of the workforce is a year of lost compounding. What happens if the market drops while you are spending down the portfolio?

What is actually true: All of this is addressed in Chapter 7 with specific numbers. The short version: the financial skeptic is calculating against the wrong baseline. They are comparing gap spending to career earning. The right comparison is gap spending to current life spending — and the gap, at $28,000 per year for two people at the documented bonusnachos level, costs significantly less than most suburban American lives. The Convenience Premium alone — $12,000 to $17,000 per year that disappears when the career ends — offsets a significant portion of the gap's apparent cost.

The financial skeptic is also ignoring the portfolio math. The couple whose portfolio generates returns that exceed a 3% to 3.5% withdrawal rate is not depleting the portfolio — they are growing it. Eric and Katie's portfolio grew 20% after inflation over five years of the gap with zero earned income. The financial skeptic is arguing from the traditional model's math. The gap's math is different.

The Timing Skeptic

What they say: Now is not the right time. The market is uncertain. The kids are not quite settled. Your parents are getting older. Wait until the conditions are better.

What is actually true: The conditions never fully arrive. The timing skeptic is describing a future that is always around the next corner — always almost right, never actually here. The children are launched but not quite independent enough. The parents are managing but you are not sure for how long. The market is uncertain but it is always uncertain.

The timing skeptic is also arguing from a particular misunderstanding of what the golden window actually is. The window is not defined by external conditions. It is defined by the alignment of internal ones — health, wealth, and time. That alignment is happening now, or it is not happening. Waiting for the external conditions to improve does not make the internal alignment last longer. It consumes it.

The stairs to the Sydney Opera House are climbable right now. They may not be in ten years. The timing skeptic is arguing for waiting until conditions are better while the window closes.

The Social Skeptic

What they say: What will you do all day? Will you not get bored? Will you not feel purposeless?

What is actually true: This is the question that reveals the most about the person asking it. The social skeptic cannot imagine a life organized around something other than work because their identity is enmeshed with their career in a way they have not examined. Research shows that when people become too disconnected from a career that forms the foundation of their identity, it can lead to depression, anxiety, and loneliness. Extended breaks allow individuals time to explore priorities and pursue interests outside of work.

The Golden Gap reader is not taking the gap to do nothing. They are taking it to do the things the career prevented — the books, the writing, the consulting, the travel, the cooking, the curiosity that has been locked in the box for thirty-five years. The social skeptic is imagining the gap as an absence. It is a presence. A different presence than the career provided, organized around different priorities, producing different outputs.

The answer to 'what will you do all day' is: everything I have not had time to do.

The Grandmother Skeptic

This is the most sympathetic type — the person who only knows one model. They are not arguing in bad faith. They are arguing from a framework that was complete and coherent for the life they lived. The traditional model worked for their generation. Work, retire, stop. The pension and the gold watch and the smaller house in Florida.

The response to the Grandmother Skeptic is not an argument. It is a demonstration. Go. Come back with the story. Let the life you built speak for itself. Most people who only know one model update their understanding when they see a better one working in real time in the life of someone they love.

My brother updated his understanding. Your grandmother would have too, eventually.

The Internal Skeptic — The Most Important One

The external skeptics are manageable. Most of them, as I discovered, are quieter than anticipated — curious more than critical, and often carrying their own unacknowledged version of the same desire.

The internal skeptic is different.

Mine is not about the decision. I know the decision was right. I can justify every angle of it and have, to myself, more times than I can count. I am intelligent. I know the information. No one else who has not done the same reading has a better position from which to evaluate the choice.

My internal skeptic is about the money.

Specifically: the impatience. Knowing the income is coming — the writing, the consulting, the content creation — and waiting for it to arrive at the scale that reduces the financial anxiety. Knowing the direction is right and not yet seeing the full confirmation. The gap between the clarity of the direction and the current state of the bank balance.

This is the Maker's specific internal skeptic. It is not doubt about the gap. It is the normal, legitimate anxiety of someone who has bet on themselves and is waiting for the bet to pay. The income will come. The traction will build. The work being done right now is the work that produces the income. The impatience is not a signal that the decision was wrong. It is the emotional experience of building something before it is built.

The internal skeptic who says I do not have enough money yet is telling the truth. The response to that truth is not to doubt the direction. It is to work. The work is what produces the income. The income is what quiets the internal skeptic. The only path from here to there runs through the work.

Every Maker knows this. Knowing it does not make the impatience go away. But it makes the impatience comprehensible rather than alarming.

There is something about travel and seeing new places that can fill you with awe and inspiration in a way that routine life does not. Your routines are self-reinforcing with your geography. If you take time off but you are going to the same coffee shop and seeing the same people, it is harder to do anything different. You have to explain yourself at every turn.

The gap removes the explaining. It removes the geography that reinforces the old routines. It creates the specific conditions in which the new thing can actually develop rather than being constantly compared to the old one.

The internal skeptic quiets when the work produces results. The first chapter that makes you smile. The first client call that goes well. The first payment from something you built rather than something you were hired to do. Not silence — reduction. The internal skeptic never fully disappears. It calibrates to the evidence.

What You Know That They Do Not

Here is the piece of this chapter that matters most.

By the time you are having the conversation with any external skeptic —

the career skeptic, the financial skeptic, the timing skeptic, the social skeptic, the grandmother skeptic — you have read this book. You have the data on the withdrawal rates and the bonusnachos numbers and the decompression research and the relationship reset and the family equation and the four stages. You know the full picture.

They do not.

They are arguing from the traditional model with the traditional model's assumptions about what is possible, what is affordable, what is responsible, and what is worth wanting. You are arguing from a different model — one built on documented evidence, not convention.

You do not need to convince them. You do not need to win the argument. You need to know the argument well enough that you are not persuaded by someone who knows less than you do.

I would not argue. I do what I want to do, and I do that because I can justify my decisions. I know all the angles and the information. No one else does.

That is not arrogance. That is the specific confidence of someone who has done the work.

You have done the work.

The skeptics have not.

That does not make their concern invalid. It makes their conclusion uninformed. There is a difference.

The Right Question

The external skeptics are asking: what if the gap does not work?

That is the wrong question.

The right question is: what does not taking the gap cost?

The Northern Lights you did not see. The stairs to the Sydney Opera House while you could still climb them. The version of your marriage that had something new at dinner. The book that was in your head for fifteen years. The curiosity that was locked in the box while the career consumed everything. The identity that was always underneath the professional performance, waiting for space to emerge.

Those are not abstract losses. They are specific, irreversible, accumulating costs — the costs of the traditional model that the external skeptics are implicitly recommending.

The real risk is not taking the gap.

The real risk is the Northern Lights that are still up there while you are still in the same bed in the same house in the same city, choosing the new project again.

CHAPTER THIRTEEN

The Gap Is a Living Laboratory

I never thought I could write a book.

Not in the abstract sense of thinking books were beyond ordinary people — I knew plenty of people who had written books. In the specific sense of genuinely not knowing whether I had the sustained capability to produce something substantive. The idea was not the problem. The sitting down and doing it every day, in the required volume and quality, over the required period of time — that was the hypothesis I had never tested.

The gap gave me the conditions to run the experiment.

The result: three books written, a fourth in progress, and the specific, earned certainty that comes not from believing you can do something but from having done it. That is a different kind of knowing. The hypothesis was tested. The result was positive. The uncertainty is gone.

But the more interesting discovery was not the result. It was the methodology. I discovered that I work just as hard for myself as I did for any employer. Harder, in some ways. Not because of obligation — I feel less obligated than I ever did when the emails arrived at 11pm and the weekend projects needed to be completed by Monday. I work because the work benefits me directly. Every hour of effort goes toward my own horizon rather than someone else's quarterly numbers. My wife, who spent years telling me that the company did not deserve fourteen hours of my day, no longer says anything when I stay up late. Not because she has given up. Because the late hours are mine now.

That was a hypothesis too. I had wondered whether I would push myself without external accountability — without the boss waiting on the plan, without the metrics that measured whether I was performing. The answer came quickly and clearly: yes. The drive that I applied to proving my value to an organization I turned, without apparent loss of intensity, toward building something for myself.

The experiment was not designed in advance. I did not sit down before the gap with a hypothesis sheet and a methodology. But looking back, that is exactly what was happening. The gap was the laboratory. The living was the experiment. The results were coming in continuously, whether I was tracking them deliberately or not.

The gap-taker who runs the experiments deliberately gets there faster.

—

What a Laboratory Actually Is

The laboratory frame is not a metaphor designed to make the gap sound scientific. It is a description of what the gap actually does when you engage with it honestly.

A laboratory is a place where you test hypotheses under controlled conditions and observe what the results actually show — not what you hoped they would show, not what you feared they would show, but what they actually show. The results are information. Good results and bad results are both useful. A failed experiment is not a failure. It is a data point that eliminates one option and points toward the next hypothesis.

Research on extended breaks from work describes them as providing a psychological safe space to change one's personal identity and to figure out what it means to live a more authentic life. The researchers found that participants progress through three stages: healing, exploring, and reintegrating.

The laboratory frame makes that process active rather than passive. You are not waiting for clarity to arrive. You are running experiments that generate it. The gap-taker who treats every experience as data — every morning that feels energizing, every project that stalls, every relationship that deepens or strains, every direction that gains traction or loses it — is running a deliberate research program on the most important subject available: their own life.

Henry Ford captured something essential about this, though the precise wording has been attributed to many people over the years. The idea is always the same: the only real mistake is the one from which you learn nothing. Failure that generates learning is not failure. It is methodology.

The gap is full of what the traditional model calls failures. Directions that did not pan out. Projects that stalled. Hypotheses that turned out to be wrong. Income that did not arrive on the timeline expected. Identity structures that turned out to be less stable than assumed.

Every one of these is laboratory data. Every one eliminates an option or refines the direction or provides new information about what the next experiment should test.

What Gets Tested in the Laboratory

The laboratory of the gap runs experiments across four dimensions simultaneously — often without the gap-taker noticing that experiments are underway.

Identity Experiments: Who Am I Without the Title?

This is the experiment that most gap-takers report as the most disorienting and ultimately the most valuable. The career provided an identity that was legible, portable, and socially understood. The title answered the party question. The organizational affiliation explained the context. The performance metrics told you, continuously, whether you were succeeding.

The gap removes all of this and replaces it with nothing — initially. The identity experiment begins in Stage One and does not fully resolve until well into Stage Three. What you discover in that experimental process is which parts of the career identity were genuinely yours and which parts were borrowed from the organization.

The person who thought their identity was their expertise discovers that the expertise is portable — it does not belong to the company that employed it. The person who thought their identity was their title discovers that the title was a container they were using to organize things that would have been there anyway. The person who thought their identity was their professional network discovers that the network was mostly professional and much of it thins when the professional context disappears.

And then — underneath all of that — something else. The curiosity that ran before the career gave it a job. The specific interests that existed before the performance metrics organized them. The version of the self that predates the professional identity.

That version is recoverable. The laboratory experiment reveals it.

Energy Experiments: What Gives Me Life and What Depletes It?

The career organized the day around what needed to be done, not around what sustained the person doing it. The result, for most gap-takers, is that they have almost no reliable data on their own energy — on which activities genuinely engage them versus which they have trained themselves to endure.

The gap provides the specific experimental conditions needed to answer this question. When the schedule is yours, what do you fill it with? When nothing is required, what do you reach for? When you have the whole canvas, where does the brush naturally go?

The energy experiments are illuminating in both directions. The gap-taker discovers which activities produce flow — the state where effort disappears and time passes without notice. Those activities are pointing toward the core of the direction worth pursuing. I found myself staying up late working on my projects, not out of obligation but out of genuine engagement. The work was interesting enough to lose track of time. That is a piece of energy data.

The experiments are also illuminating in the negative direction. The gap-taker discovers which activities they thought they wanted — the long reading days, the total absence of structure, the pure leisure — and finds, if they are honest, that some produce restlessness rather than restoration. The person who discovers they are happiest when building something has learned that pure leisure was not the destination. The laboratory needed to test the hypothesis to confirm it.

Direction Experiments: What Does It Feel Like When I Do the Work?

This is the experiment that separates the gap-taker who arrives at Stage Four with a real direction from the one who arrives with a theory.

Many people enter the gap with ideas about what they want to do next. The book they have been meaning to write. The consulting practice they have been thinking about. The creative project that has been in the back of their mind for years. The laboratory converts these from intentions into experiments.

The direction experiment is simple in design: do the work and observe what happens. Not imagine doing the work. Not plan the work. Do it and see what the doing produces — in the work itself and in the person doing it.

My direction experiment with writing produced an unexpected result. The hypothesis was that AI tools would help me make my sentences sound better. The experiment revealed something much more significant: the AI partnership taught me to ask better questions. It required me to break complex subjects into specific chunks before I could use it effectively. It forced a kind of analytical clarity — the ability to think critically when results seemed skewed, to identify what was missing, to refine the prompt until the output was actually useful — that turned out to be a capability I had not previously exercised in this form.

The writing was the direction. The AI was the tool. But the deeper result of the experiment was a new methodology for research and synthesis: taking real-world interviews and accounts of Golden Gap experiences, reading them carefully, then using AI-driven research to prove, disprove, or add depth to what the people reported. Combining human experience with verified data. Testing the anecdote against the evidence and letting the truth emerge from the combination.

That methodology is not what I came to the gap planning to develop. It emerged from running the experiment.

Relationship Experiments: What Does the Partnership Look Like with the Structure Removed?

The relationship dimension of the gap is one of the most significant experiments running, and most couples do not think of it as an experiment until they are already in it.

The hypothesis most couples bring to the gap is either hopeful or anxious. Either the gap will be a wonderful shared adventure that brings them closer, or the 24/7 togetherness will strain something previously managed by separation. Both hypotheses contain partial truth. The experiment reveals the actual proportion.

What the experiment mostly reveals, for couples whose relationship is fundamentally sound, is that the structure was doing more relationship maintenance than they realized — and that they are more capable of generating their own rhythm, their own togetherness and separateness, than the career years ever gave them the opportunity to discover. The laboratory does not tell you what you hoped to find. It tells you what is actually there.

Permission to Be Wrong

Here is the part of the laboratory frame that matters most for the gap-taker who is afraid of committing to a direction.

The laboratory gives you permission to be wrong.

Not permission to be careless or uncommitted or permanently uncertain. Permission to run an experiment, observe the result honestly, update the direction, and run the next experiment. This is how real knowledge is built — not by getting the answer right on the first try but by running enough experiments to eliminate the wrong answers and converge on the right one.

The book that does not find readers in the first year is not evidence that you cannot write. It is evidence that the marketing hypothesis needs refinement, or the audience identification needs work, or the distribution strategy is incomplete. The experiment failed. The direction is not invalidated. The next experiment gets run with better information.

The consulting practice that takes eight months to find its first client rather than two months is not evidence that the expertise has no market. It is evidence about the sales cycle, the client acquisition approach, the positioning, the pricing. The experiment ran slower than the hypothesis predicted. The data is still useful.

The gap-taker who treats every outcome as a verdict — who judges the whole enterprise by the early results before the experiments have had time to run — is using the wrong framework. Early results in any new direction are almost always worse than later results, because the methodology is still being refined, the audience is still being found, the offering is still being sharpened.

The research on people who have taken extended breaks is consistent on this point. Most of those who stayed with the direction long enough found what they were looking for. After taking a sabbatical, virtually all participants reported renewed energy, creativity, and confidence. The hard-won perspective comes from running the experiments, not from deciding in advance what the results will be.

The Spectrum of Experiments

The laboratory runs differently depending on where you are on the gap spectrum.

For the gap-taker who is financially comfortable — who has enough in the portfolio that the income question is secondary — the experiments are almost entirely in the identity, energy, and direction dimensions. What do I actually want to do? What sustains me? Who am I when I am not producing for an organization? These are the questions the laboratory is running, and the financial dimension is not creating urgency that distorts the results.

This version of the laboratory is, in some ways, the purest. The experiments run without the pressure of needing them to produce income quickly. The direction can be followed wherever it leads. The identity question can be explored fully without the anxiety of needing the answer to fund next month's expenses.

The experiments that tend to emerge in this version: travel style experiments — what kind of environment sustains versus depletes? Relationship rhythm experiments — what does the partnership want when there is no external structure? Interest experiments — which of the things I always wanted to pursue are genuinely interesting when I am actually pursuing them, and which turn out to be more romantic in imagination than in practice?

For the Maker — the gap-taker who is building something that needs to generate income within the runway — the laboratory runs with more urgency and more specific hypotheses. The experiments are about direction confirmation and income validation rather than pure exploration. Which of these possible directions has a market? What does the work feel like at the level of daily practice? What does the audience actually respond to?

This version of the laboratory is more pressured but also more focused. The need to generate results creates the specific discipline that pure exploration sometimes lacks. The Maker who knows the runway is finite runs tighter experiments, gets results faster, and updates direction more efficiently — because the stakes of running too many failed experiments are higher.

Both versions are legitimate. Both produce the information that Stage Four requires. The experiments just have different designs.

What a Completed Experiment Looks Like

The laboratory frame is more useful in practice when you can see what a completed experiment actually looks like — from hypothesis to result to updated direction.

The writing experiment:

Hypothesis: I can write books. The sustained daily practice of writing is something I can maintain without an external deadline imposing structure.

Experiment: Write the books. Actually sit down and do the work. Track what the work produces.

Result: Three books completed. A fourth in progress. The hypothesis confirmed not by aspiration but by output. The secondary discovery that AI partnership is not a shortcut but a discipline — requiring better questions, clearer thinking, more specific chunking of complex subjects.

Updated direction: Continue building the body of work. Develop the AI research methodology further. Seek the audience that is waiting for what is being built.

The self-direction experiment:

Hypothesis: I will push myself without external accountability. The drive that produced results in the career will function equally when pointed at my own work.

Experiment: Remove the external accountability structures — the boss, the metrics, the performance review — and observe what happens to the work rate.

Result: The hypothesis confirmed. The work rate is comparable to the career. The hours are longer, not shorter. The difference is the guilt. Working fourteen hours for yourself feels different from working fourteen hours for an organization — not because the hours are shorter but because the direction of the value is different. Every hour builds something that belongs to you.

Updated direction: Trust the self-direction. Stop checking whether it is still working. It is working.

The Experiment That Is Still Running

Every laboratory has experiments in progress. Questions that have not yet resolved. Hypotheses that the data is still testing.

Mine is the methodology. The combination of real-world experience and AI-driven research verification — taking what people report about their gap experience and testing it against the evidence that confirms, complicates, or deepens what they felt. Building a way of knowing that is more rigorous than personal anecdote and more human than pure data.

This experiment is still running. The results are still coming in. The book you are reading is one of its outputs.

That is what the laboratory produces when it is working properly. Not a finished answer — a better question. Not a complete direction — a refined one. Not certainty — the specific, earned confidence that comes from having tested the hypothesis rather than assumed the answer.

The gap-taker who arrives at Stage Four with data instead of guesses has run the experiments. They know what they know because they tested it. They know what they do not know because they tested that too.

That is not the end of the laboratory. The laboratory does not close when the gap ends. It just moves into the next chapter with a more sophisticated methodology and a more refined set of hypotheses.

The experiments continue. The results keep coming.

THE PRACTICE

Chapters 14 – 16

Slow travel as a way of life

CHAPTER FOURTEEN

Slow Travel: The Philosophy and the Practice

Ferris Bueller figured it out in 1986. Life moves pretty fast. If you don't stop and look around once in a while, you could miss it. He was seventeen and playing hooky from high school. You are fifty-something and have spent thirty years moving fast. The stopping and looking around part is overdue.

—

Yesterday my wife and I walked from Bondi Beach to Coogee Beach.

It is one of the most celebrated coastal walks in the world. Six kilometers of clifftop paths, ocean baths, headlands, and harbor views that have made this stretch of Sydney coastline famous enough to appear in every travel magazine that has ever written about Australia. My wife has walked it thirty times. She grew up near here. This route is exercise to her — a familiar track with a known gradient and a predictable endpoint.

She wanted to move fast. Get the heart rate up. Cover the distance.

About five minutes in, I stopped.

Below me and to the left, the full sweep of Bondi Beach opened up. Waves coming in clean lines from the south. Surfers reading the water. And perched on the cliffs above the beach, these extraordinary houses — white and angular, positioned like something placed there deliberately to make the point that some views are worth paying almost any price to wake up to. I stood there for two minutes. Maybe three. Long enough for my wife to notice I was no longer beside her.

She came back. We kept walking.

Fifteen minutes later, I stopped again.

The path ran close to the cliff edge and I looked down. Below were wide flat rocks — volcanic, I think, worn to a horizontal smoothness by ten thousand years of tide. The water came in, washed across the surface, and as it slid back off the edge into the ocean it went flat and still for just a moment — a brief, impossible sheet of glass before the next wave arrived. I watched it happen four or five times. Each time the same. Each time different.

She came back. We kept walking.

Thirty minutes later, I stopped a third time.

The path curved around a headland and the ocean opened up to the east, fully exposed, nothing between us and New Zealand. The waves here were serious — deep water swells that had been building for a thousand kilometers and arrived with no warning and complete commitment. Each one hit the rocks below and sent water twenty feet into the air. Not a spray. A column. A brief white vertical explosion that hung for a second before gravity decided.

I watched for a while.

My wife walked back to me and told me we did not have time to watch the waves. We needed to move faster to get the exercise.

I looked at her and asked if she knew who Ferris Bueller was.

She is not from the United States. The reference did not land the way it lands for someone who was sixteen in 1986 and watched Matthew Broderick freeze time in a Chicago art museum while Yello played on the soundtrack. I tried to explain. I told her that we were getting older. That life moves fast. That we needed to stop and look around more than we had been.

She mumbled something and started walking again.

I stood there another thirty seconds watching the water go twenty feet into the air.

Then I followed her.

—

That walk is this chapter.

My wife has moved along this route thirty times and knows it as exercise. I moved along it once and saw it as a place. Neither of us is wrong. But only one of us stopped three times.

The difference between a tourist and a slow traveler is not how many countries they visit. It is not how long they stay. It is not even whether they speak the language or cook at home or know the name of the café on the corner.

It is whether they stop.

Slow travel is not a pace. It is a practice. It is the deliberate cultivation of presence in a place — the decision to inhabit rather than consume, to notice rather than collect, to be somewhere fully rather than move through it efficiently.

The Golden Gap is built for this. Not because the itinerary is slower. Because the life is.

What Slow Travel Is Not

Before defining what slow travel is, let me clear the ground.

Slow travel is not a long vacation. A vacation is recovery from a life you return to unchanged. You can take a three-week vacation and move through every day at tourist pace — maximizing sights, hitting the highlights, returning home with photographs and a vague sense of having been somewhere. The speed is different from a weekend trip. The quality of presence is identical.

Slow travel is not extended tourism. Extended tourism is what happens when you take vacation logic — maximize, cover, collect, move — and apply it over a longer period. The couple who does five countries in four months is not slow traveling. They are vacationing for longer. The distinction matters because extended tourism produces the wall. The templed-out moment. The exhaustion of perpetual novelty that arrives around month four and makes a person question everything.

Slow travel is not retirement. It is not the absence of purpose or the abandonment of ambition. The slow traveler is not drifting. They are inhabiting. There is a significant difference between someone who has stopped moving and someone who has stopped rushing.

And slow travel is not what my wife was doing on the Bondi to Coogee walk. Not because she was wrong to want exercise — the body needs what it needs — but because she had walked the route thirty times and the familiarity had made it invisible. Familiarity is the enemy of presence. When we know a place, we stop seeing it. We move through the map of it in our heads rather than the reality of it under our feet.

One of the gifts the Golden Gap gives you is the unfamiliar. A place you have never been, moving at a pace that lets you see it before it becomes familiar. The glass water on the volcanic rock. The twenty-foot column of ocean against the headland. The houses on the cliff that someone decided were worth everything.

You cannot see these things at exercise pace. You can only see them if you stop.

The Vacation Logic Problem

Here is what almost everyone does in the first months of extended travel.

They travel the way they vacationed.

It makes complete sense. Vacationing is the only frame most people have for being somewhere that is not home. You have done it dozens of times. You know how it works. You arrive, you orient, you identify the things worth seeing, you see them, you move to the next location, you repeat. The logic is efficient. It maximizes the ratio of sights to days. It produces a satisfying sense of coverage.

It is completely wrong for the Golden Gap.

One couple who has been slow traveling for eight years described their first four months with uncomfortable honesty. They had started in Southeast Asia. Five countries in four months. Constantly on the go. And then around month four they hit the wall. Templed out, they called it. Wanted the comforts of home. Questioning everything. The novelty threshold had risen so high that nothing registered anymore. Each new temple, each new market, each new city produced less feeling than the one before. The stimulation machine had run out of stimulation.

They stopped. Stayed in one place for a week. Had the conversation about what they actually wanted. And then they did something that changed everything.

They slowed down.

Four weeks minimum in any location became their rule. Not because the guidebook recommended it. Because experience taught them that four weeks is approximately how long it takes for a place to stop being a destination and start being a place you live. The first week you are a tourist. The second week you are a visitor. The third week you are a temporary resident. The fourth week you are, in some small but real sense, a local. You have a coffee shop. You have a route. You have a face that the market vendor recognizes. You have begun to understand the rhythms of the neighborhood rather than the attractions of the city.

There is a name for what happened to them. Economists call it the law of diminishing marginal utility. The ice cream cone version is easier to remember.

Eat two ice cream cones and you enjoyed them both. The second was slightly less transcendent than the first, but you would absolutely do it again. Eat seven and somewhere around cone four the pleasure starts becoming obligation. By cone seven you are not tasting ice cream. You are managing a situation.

The temple at month one was extraordinary. The temple at month four was another temple.

Not because Southeast Asia ran out of extraordinary temples. Because the nervous system recalibrated. The instrument adjusted to the new input level and required more and more stimulation to produce the same response. The first cone is always the best one. The seventh is just filling you up.

Fast travel — constant movement, perpetual novelty, new city every few days

— is eating seven cones in a row. The Base Camp Model is eating one cone slowly, going for a walk, and discovering the next day that the first bite tastes like the first bite again.

The four-week minimum is not an arbitrary rule. It is the time it takes for the instrument to reset between cones.

The vacation logic problem is not a character flaw. It is a software issue. You arrive running the wrong operating system. The Golden Gap requires an upgrade.

The upgrade takes time and usually requires hitting the wall first. The book's job is to tell you the wall is coming so that when it arrives you recognize it as the upgrade process beginning rather than evidence that the whole decision was a mistake.

The Base Camp Model

The most practical and financially powerful framework for slow travel is what I call the Base Camp Model.

A base camp, in mountaineering, is not where the adventure happens. It is what makes the adventure sustainable. The fixed point. The resupply station. The place you return to after each push, where you recover, restock, and prepare for the next one.

The Base Camp Model for slow travel works exactly the same way.

You rent a monthly apartment in one city — your hub. From that fixed address you make day trips, overnight excursions, and regional explorations — the spokes. When the month or two is complete, you pick up everything and move the hub to a new location. A new continent, a new climate, a new set of spokes radiating outward from a new center.

This model solves five problems simultaneously.

The financial problem. Monthly rentals run 40 to 50% cheaper than the same property booked nightly. On a $100 per night apartment, that is $1,200 to $1,500 saved per month before you account for anything else. Add the kitchen dividend — two people cooking most meals at home from local markets rather than eating out for every meal — and you save another $1,500 to $2,500 per month compared to restaurant-dependent travel. The Base Camp Model is not a budget compromise. It is a financial strategy.

The transport problem. When you move every few days, you buy flights constantly. When you operate from a hub, you buy one arrival flight and one departure flight per hub. Everything in between is regional — trains, buses, budget carriers for $20 to $60, or simply not needed because the day trips return to your own bed. One couple documented a full year in Europe visiting thirteen cities across eight countries with zero flights and a total transport cost of $1,023. Not per month. For the year. The no-airport year is not a constraint. It is what happens when you stop moving for the sake of moving.

The cognitive problem. Every hotel check-in, every new navigation, every departure requires mental energy. Constant movement is exhausting in ways that do not appear in a spreadsheet but absolutely appear in the experience of the gap. When you have a base camp, you know where the supermarket is. You know which café has the good coffee. You know how the shower works and which key opens which lock and where the light switches are. That accumulated local knowledge is not a small thing. It is the difference between living somewhere and perpetually arriving somewhere.

The depth problem. From a hub in Lisbon you can reach Sintra, Évora, the Alentejo, the Algarve coast, Porto, and the Douro Valley — all by train or a short drive, all returning to your own bed that night. You see more of Portugal in two months from a Lisbon apartment than most tourists see in two weeks of moving daily between cities. The Base Camp Model resolves the false choice between staying put and seeing a region. It allows both simultaneously.

The relationship problem. For couples, the base camp reduces one of the primary sources of travel friction — the constant joint decision-making about logistics. Where are we going tomorrow? How do we get there? Where do we eat? When there is a home base, many of these decisions disappear or become routine. The couple can also separate more naturally — one person exploring while the other reads in the apartment or works on a project — in a way that constant hotel movement makes difficult. More on this in Chapter 10.

Choosing Your Base Camp

Not every city makes an equally good base camp. The qualities that matter are different from the qualities that make a city worth visiting as a tourist.

Regional connectivity. The best base camps are cities from which a significant region is accessible by ground transport. Lisbon reaches the whole of Portugal and parts of Spain. Chiang Mai reaches northern Thailand, Laos, and Myanmar. Medellín reaches the coffee region, the Pacific coast, and the Andes. You are not just choosing a city. You are choosing a region.

Monthly rental market. Some cities have abundant, well-priced monthly rental inventory. Others are dominated by short-stay tourism accommodation that is expensive and poorly equipped for actual living. Before committing to a base camp, search Airbnb with monthly dates and compare the inventory. A city with a deep monthly rental market is a city where locals also rent, which means the accommodation is built for living rather than visiting.

Walkability and daily infrastructure. You will spend most of your time at the base camp between excursions. The quality of the daily life — the markets, the coffee shops, the parks, the street life, the ability to get what you need without a car — matters more than the tourist attractions. A great apartment in a walkable neighborhood beats a mediocre apartment near the famous sights.

Air quality. This is worth checking before you commit. Air quality index above 100 has measurable health effects — sinus irritation, fatigue, reduced respiratory function. For the 50+ reader managing any respiratory condition, this moves from preference to necessity. IQAir.com provides current and historical AQI data by city. Some otherwise excellent base camp cities — parts of Southeast Asia in burning season, certain Latin American cities in winter — have air quality issues worth knowing about before you arrive.

City center versus satellite town. Try both. City center living gives you walkability, energy, and immediate access to culture. Satellite town living gives you quieter rhythms, lower cost, and the experience of how residents actually live. Potsdamer Platz is magnificent and after a month you start wanting Potsdam. The transit-connected satellite town is often 20 to 40% cheaper than the city center equivalent while remaining 30 to 40 minutes from everything. Sintra and Cascais are cheaper than central Lisbon. Potsdam is cheaper than central Berlin. The satellite town is worth one experiment.

The Four-Week Minimum

Four weeks is the minimum meaningful stay.

Not because the guidebook says so. Because the experiential data from every long-term slow traveler points to the same conclusion. One week is a tourist. Two weeks is an extended tourist. Three weeks is the beginning of something. Four weeks is where the place starts to reveal itself.

In the first week you are orienting. Finding the layout, the transport, the basics. You are managing the practical and the logistical. You are still in arrival mode even if you arrived four days ago.

In the second week the orientation settles and the exploration begins. You start going beyond the obvious. The neighborhood reveals its texture. You find the good market and the bad one. You discover that the café on the corner is excellent and the one across the street is not.

In the third week something shifts. The place becomes less effortful. You move through it with the ease of someone who belongs there provisionally. You have regulars. You have preferences. You have opinions about the neighborhood that a tourist would not have.

In the fourth week you are living there. Temporarily, impermanently, with full awareness that you are leaving — but living there. The difference in quality of experience between week one and week four is not incremental. It is categorical.

One experienced slow traveler with eight years of nomadic retirement put it plainly: the longer we travel, the more importance we place on staying long enough that a city becomes somewhere we live rather than somewhere we visit. He went further — he now believes that a great apartment in a mediocre city beats a mediocre apartment in a great city. The apartment is not where you sleep. It is where you live. Most of your time is spent there. Its quality has an outsized effect on everything.

Book the month. It is almost always cheaper. And it is always better.

The Rhythm of a Slow Travel Day

The question people ask most often about slow travel is some version of: but what do you actually do all day?

It is a reasonable question. The tourist version of travel is organized around activities — sights to visit, restaurants to eat at, experiences to collect. Remove the checklist and what remains?

More than you expect. And different from what you expect.

A typical base camp day does not look like a vacation day. It looks more like a good day at home — but in a more interesting place, with more freedom, and without the background radiation of obligations and urgency that made the good days at home rare.

You wake without an alarm. You make coffee in your own kitchen from beans you bought at the market two days ago. You eat breakfast at the table by the window where, if you chose well, there is something worth looking at. You read for an hour, or write, or do whatever the project of the Golden Gap requires from you that morning.

Around mid-morning you go out. Not to see a sight. To be in the neighborhood. You walk somewhere you have not been yet, or somewhere you want to go again. You stop when something is worth stopping for — the volcanic rock with the glass water, the waves crashing twenty feet high, the view of the houses on the cliff. You let the pace be the pace of genuine interest rather than the pace of an itinerary.

You come back for lunch, or you eat somewhere along the way. In the afternoon you might explore further, or take a day trip to somewhere in the region, or simply sit in a square and watch the city go about its life. You cook dinner from the market or you go out, depending on what the evening calls for. You do not feel guilty about either choice.

The rhythm has structure without rigidity. It has direction without urgency. It is the daily version of the Golden Gap's larger promise — a life organized around presence rather than performance.

The Download Conversation

There is one specific practice that couples doing the Golden Gap need to build in deliberately, and it is so simple that most people overlook it entirely.

Think about what your dinner table conversation looked like when you were both employed.

You sat down at the end of the day and told each other things. What happened in the meeting. What your colleague said. What you saw on the commute. What made you laugh, what frustrated you, what you noticed that the other person was not there to see. It was not small talk. It was the daily renewal of your interest in each other's separate world. You were, every evening, a source of something new to the person across the table.

The Golden Gap removes the structure that made that possible. Both of you are present for everything. The download conversation has nothing to download because nothing happened to either of you that the other did not witness.

The solution is simple and it connects directly to the Base Camp Model's flexibility.

Separate outings. At least once a week — ideally more — each person goes somewhere the other does not. Not because the relationship needs distance. Because the relationship needs material. She goes to the market you have already seen. You go to the neighborhood she has not yet explored. She takes the cooking class. You take the photography walk with the local guide. You come back to dinner with something to tell each other that the other one missed.

Watch them lean in.

You have been doing this for thirty years at the dinner table at home. The employed life provided the structure automatically. The Golden Gap requires you to build it deliberately.

Build it deliberately. It is one of the most important design decisions in the entire gap.

The Return Visit

One of the things that experienced slow travelers discover — usually in year two or three — is that the second visit to a place is qualitatively different from the first.

The first visit is exploration. You are learning the place, building your map, discovering what it is and whether you like it.

The second visit is homecoming. You already know where the good coffee is. You already know which neighborhood fits you and which one does not. You arrive not as a stranger but as someone returning to somewhere they have already chosen. The ease of it, the specific pleasure of recognized familiarity in a foreign place, is one of the quiet joys of slow travel that no travel magazine photograph captures.

After five years of nomadic retirement, one couple described their travel pattern this way: they have identified four cities they love and rotate among them, staying two to three months in each. They return to familiar places rather than perpetually seeking new ones. The research is lower. The arrival is easier. The quality of experience is higher.

This is not the travel that Instagram celebrates. It is the travel that actually sustains.

The perpetual novelty model — a new place every few weeks, always somewhere different, always accumulating new experiences — is exciting for a while and exhausting eventually. The slow travel model — a smaller number of places known deeply, returned to seasonally, inhabited with the ease of provisional belonging — is the model that people are still living happily eight years in.

Give yourself permission to go back.

The first temple is extraordinary. The seventh is another temple. Slow travel is the art of always being at the first one.

The Numbers

Slow travel is not just philosophically superior to fast travel. It is financially superior.

The numbers from five years of documented nomadic retirement across four continents are worth stating plainly.

Average annual spend for two people: $28,050. That is $2,337 per month. For two people. Across four continents and nineteen countries including Europe, Southeast Asia, and Latin America.

The most expensive year — which included a broken wrist requiring five doctor visits, three x-rays, and two casts, significant dental work, and the worst stock market performance since the 1930s — came in at $31,100. That is $85 per day for two people in Europe, eating well, renting comfortable apartments, traveling across eight countries and thirteen cities.

The breakdown of where that money went in the European year tells the story of the Base Camp Model in numbers. Housing was 46% of total spend at $1,197 per month. Food was 21% at $554 per month — almost entirely home cooking from local markets. Health and insurance combined was 11% at $276 per month. Transport was 3% at $85 per month for an entire year with zero flights.

Transport was 3%.

That number is the Base Camp Model in a single statistic. When you stop moving for the sake of moving, when you choose ground transport over air, when your hub does the work of keeping you close to everything you want to see — transport becomes almost irrelevant as a budget line.

Compare this to a couple spending $80,000 per year in suburban America. The same financial resources that fund a suburban American lifestyle fund three years of the Golden Gap at these spending levels. The same portfolio that needs to be $2 million to fund traditional retirement at $80,000 per year needs to be $700,000 to fund the Golden Gap at $28,000 per year.

Geographic arbitrage combined with the Base Camp Model does not just make travel affordable. It makes it financially superior to staying home.

The Convenience Premium

There is a financial shift that happens during the Golden Gap that most people do not anticipate. It is not about budgeting or frugality. It is about a question that flips.

During the career years, time was your scarce resource. Money bought it back. You ordered delivery because you did not have time to cook. You hired the cleaner because you did not have time to clean. You outsourced the lawn, the errands, the grocery run, the meal planning — all of it justified by the same calculation: time is scarce, money is more available, spend the money and recover the time.

The Convenience Premium — the annual total of everything a suburban couple spends specifically to buy back time — runs $12,000 to $17,000 per year. Restaurant meals above home-cook cost: $6,000 to $8,000. Food delivery fees and markups: $1,500 to $2,000. Grocery delivery charges: $600 to $1,000. House cleaning: $1,500 to $2,400. Lawn care: $1,200 to $2,000. Miscellaneous convenience services: $1,000 to $1,500. None of this is waste. All of it was rational given the constraints. You were not being lazy. You were being time-poor.

The Golden Gap removes the constraints. Time is no longer scarce. The Convenience

Premium does not just shrink during the Golden Gap. It largely disappears — not because you become austere or disciplined but because the life structure that generated the need for it no longer exists. There is no lawn. There is no car. There is no commute. The groceries are at a market three minutes from your apartment that you enjoy visiting because it is interesting and because you have nowhere else to be.

The question flips. During the career: is this worth the time it saves? During the Golden Gap: is this worth the money it costs? Same transaction. Opposite question. Different answer almost every time.

Cooking at home during the career felt like a burden because it consumed scarce time. Cooking at home in Lisbon or Chiang Mai or Medellín is not a burden. Shopping at the local market, figuring out the cheese counter in Vienna, learning to navigate the covered market in Chiang Mai — these are not chores that reduce the convenience of your day. They are experiences that are the substance of your day. The cooking is not a compromise on the restaurant experience. It is a different and frequently richer experience.

This is also why the $554 per month food figure in Eric and Katie's European year is not a deprivation number. It is a quality-of-life number. Almost entirely home cooking from local markets. Fresh produce, local cheese, good bread, whatever looked interesting at the stall that morning. No delivery fees. No restaurant markup. No tip. Just two people with time and curiosity and a kitchen, eating very well for $277 each per month.

The Convenience Premium is the hidden cost of a time-poor life. The Golden Gap is its dissolution.

Slow Travel and Your Body

One more thing worth naming before this chapter closes.

Slow travel is quietly, continuously, and measurably better for your body than the suburban lifestyle it replaces.

Not because you join a gym. Because you live in walkable places and your days are unscheduled and the world outside your door is interesting. You walk to the market.

You walk to the café. You walk the Bondi to Coogee coastal path and stop three times to look at things that are worth stopping for.

A writer who tracked his biometric data through a career sabbatical found that his daily step count was higher during slow travel than at any point in his working life. Not from exercise. From daily life in places built for pedestrians rather than cars.

On the Bondi to Coogee walk, my wife was getting exercise. I was getting exercise and something else. I was getting the specific physical experience of moving through a place slowly enough to see it. The cardiovascular benefit was identical. The experiential benefit was not.

The slow traveler walks more, stresses less, sleeps better in unfamiliar beds than in familiar ones, and returns from the day energized rather than depleted. Not because slow travel is a health program. Because it is a life organized around presence rather than performance, and the body responds to that distinction in ways the biometric data makes impossible to argue with.

The Philosophy and the Practice

Slow travel is not a technique. It is a philosophy that produces techniques.

The philosophy is this: a place reveals itself to those who stay long enough to see it. The depth of an experience is inversely proportional to the speed at which you move through it. Presence is not a natural state in a world organized around efficiency — it is a deliberate practice that requires design, protection, and the occasional willingness to stop on a clifftop path and watch waves crash into rocks while the person next to you tells you there is no time.

There is always time.

That is the point.

Ferris Bueller skipped school on a Tuesday and stood in front of a Seurat painting at the Art Institute of Chicago and really looked at it — at the dots that made up the image, at the way meaning assembled itself from what seemed like chaos up close — and understood something about presence that most people spend a lifetime missing.

You are not skipping school. You are taking the Golden Gap.

But the instruction is the same.

Stop and look around.

The view from the cliff above Bondi Beach is extraordinary. The volcanic rock with the glass water is extraordinary. The twenty-foot column of ocean against the headland is extraordinary.

You will not see any of it at exercise pace.

Five Honest Reflections

One: The first weeks of slow travel will feel like vacation. That is not what they are. Give it time. The vacation logic takes approximately four months to shed. The wall is not a failure. It is the upgrade process beginning.

Two: The Base Camp Model is not a compromise between travel and stability. It is the discovery that stability is what makes travel sustainable. One apartment, one neighborhood, one set of rhythms — from which you reach everything within range.

Three: The four-week minimum is not a rule. It is what the data from every experienced slow traveler consistently shows. One week you are a tourist. Four weeks you are living there. The difference is not incremental. It is categorical.

Four: Build the separate outing into your week deliberately. Not because the relationship needs distance. Because it needs material. Have something to tell each other that the other one missed. You have been doing this for thirty years. You just did not know that was what you were doing.

Five: Go back to the places you love. The perpetual novelty model is exciting for a season and exhausting eventually. The return visit is one of the quiet joys of slow travel that nothing else replicates. Give yourself permission to already have favorites.

CHAPTER FIFTEEN

The Entry Point

There are 195 countries in the world.

Approximately 70 of them have nomad visas, retirement visa programs, or visa-free entry for American passport holders that make slow travel legally and practically straightforward. Of those 70, several dozen have established expat and slow travel communities, reliable monthly rental markets, walkable cities, and the infrastructure a 50-plus gap-taker actually needs.

That is a lot of options.

Too many options, without a framework for choosing between them, produces a specific kind of paralysis. The gap-taker who spends six months researching destinations before committing to any of them is not being thorough. They are postponing a decision by turning the research into the project. The research is not the gap. The gap is the gap. At some point you have to go somewhere.

This chapter gives you the framework and then makes the recommendation.

We are in Australia right now. That is the opening of the personal entry point and also the explanation for why Australia is not where this chapter tells you to go first — unless you have family there and someone whose house you can stay in while they travel, which is exactly how we ended up here and exactly what made it work. The family connection brought us. The home exchange saved us real money. The position of Australia as a major international hub — planes from everywhere fly in, and from Australia you can fly to everywhere — made it an ideal launching pad for what comes next.

But Australia runs American prices. If the gap's financial model requires geographic arbitrage to work, Australia is not the place to deploy it. Portugal is. Chiang Mai is. Medellín is. Australia is a wonderful place to visit family and use someone else's house for six weeks. It is not the slow travel value proposition.

For most readers, the entry point is somewhere else. Here is how to find yours.

—

The Base Camp Selection Framework

Before the regional recommendations, the framework. Because the right framework applied to any city produces a better answer than the best recommendation applied without understanding why.

Walkability

This is the single most important criterion for the 50-plus slow traveler and the one most commonly underweighted. A walkable base camp turns movement into pleasure rather than logistics. It provides the automatic daily exercise that Stage One decompression requires. It eliminates the car dependency that inflates costs and creates stress. And it ensures that the market, the coffee shop, the restaurant, the pharmacy, and the park are reachable without a car or a ride order every time you need them. Walk Score exists for a reason. Use it.

Monthly Rental Availability

The base camp model depends on monthly rentals at 40 to 50% below nightly rates. Before committing to a city, verify that monthly rentals in furnished apartments with kitchens actually exist at the price point you need. Some cities are primarily tourist destinations with only nightly pricing. Some have robust monthly markets that serve exactly the slow traveler demographic. The difference between these two categories is the difference between $1,200 a month and $4,500 a month for the same apartment. Research the monthly rental market specifically — Airbnb monthly filters, Furnished Finder, Facebook expat groups, and local property listing sites.

English Proficiency

This matters more than most travel writers will tell you. The reality of daily slow travel life — the landlord conversation, the pharmacy, the bank, the internet provider, the doctor — is that you will have dozens of practical interactions in the local language every week. High English proficiency in the local population makes those interactions navigable. Portugal scores very high. Spain scores high. Thailand scores moderate — high in tourist areas, lower elsewhere. Eastern European countries vary significantly by city and generation.

Healthcare Access

The 50-plus traveler needs to think about this more carefully than the 30-year-old digital nomad. What is the quality of the private hospital system? Is there an English-speaking doctor available? What does an emergency look like at 2am? Budapest has excellent private healthcare at a fraction of Western prices. Lisbon has strong public and private options. Chiang Mai has internationally accredited private hospitals where a consultation costs $30. Medellín has modern private clinics with English-speaking staff. Research specific to your health needs before committing.

Regional Connectivity

The base camp model works because the city is a hub, not a destination. You live in Lisbon and day trip to Sintra, Évora, the Alentejo coast. You live in Chiang Mai and day trip to Doi Inthanon, Chiang Rai, the hill tribe villages. The base camp should have excellent regional connectivity — easy trains, cheap domestic flights, reliable bus systems — so that the day trips and two-night excursions are genuinely accessible rather than complicated expeditions.

The Expat Community

Not because you want to spend all your time with other Americans, but because an established expat community is evidence that the infrastructure works for people like you. They have figured out the monthly rental market, the banking workaround, the good doctor, the best market, the neighborhood to avoid. Their knowledge is freely shared in Facebook groups and expat forums and at the coffee shop where they tend to cluster. Arrive into an established community and you compress the orientation curve from three months to three weeks.

The Regions — Experience, Character, and Honest Caveats

Chapter 7 covered the costs. This section covers the feel — what it is actually like to live in each region as a 50-plus slow traveler, not what it is like to visit for two weeks as a tourist.

Western Europe — Portugal, Spain, the South of France

The argument for starting in Western Europe is the argument for starting somewhere familiar enough to find your footing. Modern infrastructure. First-world healthcare. English widely understood. Food culture that is extraordinary and immediately accessible. Credit cards accepted everywhere. Streets lit the way streets should be lit.

Portugal ranks 7th safest globally on the 2025 Global Peace Index, with crime generally low and non-violent, and 83% of residents reporting they feel safe walking alone at night. That is not a travel brochure statistic — it is the experience of walking Lisbon at midnight and feeling like you are in a safe European city, which you are.

Western Europe is expensive relative to the rest of the slow travel world. Lisbon, which was the value play of European slow travel for years, has been discovered. Monthly rents in walkable Lisbon neighborhoods now run €1,200 to €1,800 for a furnished one-bedroom. Porto and smaller Portuguese cities run significantly lower. Spain offers genuine value in Valencia, Seville, and the smaller cities away from Madrid and Barcelona.

The honest caveat about Western Europe: it is full of people who have figured out that visitors have money and are happy to relieve them of it creatively. This is not specific to Western Europe — it is universal in tourist-heavy areas. Stay in residential neighborhoods rather than tourist zones. Shop at the local supermarket rather than the convenience store adjacent to the cathedral. Eat where the locals eat rather than where the menus are in six languages. The locals are not paying tourist prices. You do not have to either.

The other honest caveat: the romantic fantasy of the country estate or the village farmhouse does not match the reality for most gap-takers. Roads in rural European areas are often narrow, poorly marked, and genuinely difficult without a car. The charming village is charming and also 45 minutes from the nearest grocery store. The slow travel model works best in walkable cities or well-connected towns with public transport. The countryside is for day trips, not for base camp selection, unless you have a car, high tolerance for logistics, and a budget that supports it.

Southeast Asia — Thailand, Vietnam, Malaysia

Southeast Asia is where the gap-taker discovers that the financial model they thought was ambitious is actually conservative. The same apartment that costs €1,400 a month in Lisbon rents for $600 in Chiang Mai with a pool and a gym and a cleaner included.

The food is extraordinary. Fresh, complex, intensely flavorful, and available at every price point from $1 street stall to $15 restaurant. The climate is warm year-round in most of the region. The people are genuinely hospitable in a way that is cultural rather than performed.

The honest caveat about Southeast Asia — and this one matters enough to spend time on because the travel guides gloss over it: the hygiene and food preparation standards are genuinely different. When you need to use everything you have to survive, you learn to use everything. Parts of the animal that a Western butcher discards are the main ingredient here. Cooking methods that would raise flags in a Western health inspection are standard practice at a market stall. This is not a criticism — it is a description of a different relationship with food and resources. The

50-plus traveler whose digestive system has been calibrated to Western food preparation standards will experience an adjustment period. Most people adjust within two to three weeks. Some have a harder time. Go in knowing this.

The other honest caveat: Chiang Mai's burning season from February to April produces some of the worst air quality on the planet. If you have respiratory concerns, plan around it. Vietnam's Da Nang and Hoi An offer similar value without the seasonal air quality issue. Malaysia's Penang is another strong alternative — English widely spoken, extraordinary food culture, excellent healthcare, and safety scores comparable to Portugal.

For the gap-taker willing to embrace genuine difference, Southeast Asia first produces the fastest Stage Two opening. The curiosity box does not open slowly here. It opens all at once.

Latin America — Colombia, Mexico, Panama

Latin America's primary advantage for North American gap-takers is the time zone. The Maker taking client calls, the consultant maintaining any US relationship, the content creator whose audience is American — all benefit from a time zone that keeps you synchronized with the people you need to stay in contact with.

Medellín has transformed in ways that still surprise people who remember its reputation. The metro is clean and efficient. The neighborhoods of El Poblado and Laureles are genuinely walkable, genuinely safe, and genuinely beautiful. The coffee culture is extraordinary. The climate earns its description — eternal spring at 72 degrees year-round.

The honest caveat about Latin America: it is hot and humid outside the high-altitude cities like Medellín and Bogotá, and the economic inequality is visible in a way that requires psychological adjustment for most Americans. Staying in established expat neighborhoods is practical advice, not snobbery — these are the areas with the infrastructure, the safety, and the rental market that slow travel requires. The people are warm and entrepreneurial and genuinely welcoming. They are also, in tourist areas, well-practiced at identifying visitors with more money than local context. This is not malice. It is commerce. Keep the same alertness you would maintain in any unfamiliar urban environment, make friends with the people who go to work every morning, and you will be fine.

Mexico offers proximity — the easiest border crossing, the most accessible family visits, the most familiar food. San Miguel de Allende, Oaxaca City, and the Yucatán Peninsula all have established expat communities with functioning slow travel infrastructure. Panama's Pensionado visa program is the most generous retiree visa structure in the region, offering significant discounts on everything from restaurants to utilities to medical care.

Eastern Europe — Hungary, Georgia, Serbia, Albania

Eastern Europe is the value proposition that Western Europe offered a decade ago, and it is genuinely exceptional for the gap-taker whose budget is the primary constraint.

The honest caveat here is the most important thing this chapter can tell you about the region: Eastern Europe is not Western Europe at a discount. It is a genuinely different experience shaped by a genuinely different history. Many of the countries that make up the affordable Eastern European slow travel circuit spent decades under Soviet influence, and that history is visible in the infrastructure. Plumbing that runs along interior walls rather than inside them. Windows that do not quite seal. Grocery stores stocked with one brand of everything rather than four. Hotels that were considered nice in 1965 and have not been significantly updated since.

This is not universal — Budapest's newer buildings and Tbilisi's renovated old city neighborhoods are genuinely comfortable. But the expectation management required for Eastern Europe is different from what is required for Lisbon or Chiang Mai. What Eastern Europe provides that nowhere else matches: extraordinary food cultures, genuine history at every turn, prices that make the gap's math work even on a Just Enough budget, and the specific pleasure of being somewhere that has not yet been optimized for the tourist experience.

The Universal Rule

Before the recommendation, the one piece of advice that applies in every region, every city, every neighborhood on earth.

Keep to the well-lit streets. Do not act like a fool — because if you do, you will be treated like one. And make friends with the people who go to work every morning.

The person who lives in a place rather than visiting it, who knows the neighbors, who greets the market vendor by name, who is recognized at the coffee shop — that person is not a target. They are a neighbor. The slow travel model produces this kind of local embeddedness automatically, given time. The tourist who is there for four days and does not bother learning the rhythm of the place is the one who ends up in the wrong situation at the wrong time.

The reality of most places outside the United States is that daily life operates on a thinner margin than what most Americans are accustomed to. The infrastructure is older. The safety net is weaker. The gap between the comfortable expat life and the surrounding economic reality is visible in ways it is not in an American suburb. None of this should scare anyone away from their dreams. It should inform how they show up when they get there.

The Recommendation

Here is the question I would ask a 55-year-old American couple with $800,000 in savings, reasonable health, no specific language skills, and six months to spend.

How experimental are you?

If the answer is we want to get genuinely out of the box — if both people are willing to be uncomfortable, to navigate the genuinely unfamiliar, to embrace the kind of culture shock that produces the fastest Stage Two opening — go to Southeast Asia first. Vietnam or Thailand. The discomfort is real and it is temporary. The adjustment happens within weeks. And on the other side of the adjustment is a life that costs $1,400 a month, feeds you extraordinarily well, and operates at a pace that has no equivalent in Western experience. If you hate where you are staying, the money you saved on accommodation can fund a much nicer hotel than anything equivalent in Europe at the same price. The downside of Southeast Asia first is manageable. The upside is transformative.

If the answer is we are cautious and want to find our footing before we go deep — go to Spain first. Specifically: Valencia, Seville, or the Basque Country. Not Madrid or Barcelona, which are expensive and tourist-saturated. A real city with a real residential neighborhood, a real market, a real monthly rental with a kitchen. Modern infrastructure. Spanish that requires some navigation but is forgiving of beginners. Healthcare that works. A culture genuinely different from American life without being so different that it overwhelms the Stage One decompression process.

Spend a month in Spain. Get comfortable being uncomfortable at the level Spain provides. Then ask yourself the question again. One month of slow travel in a real city almost always produces a different answer than the answer given before departure. Most people who start cautious end the first month ready to go further.

One further thing. Go where you want to go. Not where this chapter tells you to go — where you have been wanting to go, in the back of your mind, for years. The gap is not a checklist. It is permission. The city

that has been calling you for a decade
deserves to be answered. Start there.

Change your mind after arriving if it is not
right. The gap is long enough to course-
correct.

CHAPTER SIXTEEN

The Weekly Architecture

Nobody warns you about the freedom problem.

The career had a structure. Not a good structure — a demanding one, often an oppressive one, organized around someone else's priorities and someone else's calendar. But it was structure. The day had a shape. Monday was different from Thursday. Morning had a different quality from afternoon. The week moved from beginning to end with a logic that was externally imposed but internally legible.

The gap removes all of it.

For most gap-takers this feels, initially, entirely good. The absence of the alarm, the inbox, the standing meeting, the performance review — all of it dissolving into open calendar and open day. The liberation of it is real and it is significant and it is exactly what Stage One decompression requires.

But then something quieter happens.

The days that are entirely open can begin to blur into each other. Not immediately — the first weeks are too intoxicating for blur. But somewhere in the second month, if nothing is organizing the week, the gap-taker can find themselves arriving at Sunday with a sense that the week was full and somehow also slightly undefined. That the project got some hours but not the sustained attention it needed. That the city got some exploring but not the depth that slow travel is supposed to provide. That the relationship got the proximity but not the specific quality of connection that the download conversation produces.

This is not failure. It is the natural result of having removed external structure without replacing it with anything.

The chapter is not about recreating the career's schedule. It is about designing the minimum architecture that gives the week enough shape to hold both the work and the world — and then staying light enough inside that architecture to stop and watch a boat go by in the harbor when one comes along.

—

What a Week Actually Looks Like

We are in Australia right now. The week
has found a rhythm that was not planned
— it emerged from paying attention to
what the days actually want.

Two or three days are work days. Mornings
at the laptop, mostly. Personal emails and
texts checked in bed first, then reading
together for a while — one of the small
pleasures of a morning that is not
organized around a 7am call. Work starts
when it starts. The book, the research, the
AI tools open and running. By early
afternoon the work has done what it is
going to do for the day.

Around 2pm we go out.

Not because 2pm is scheduled as the
departure time. Because that is when the
morning's work has a natural stopping
point and the afternoon light in this part of
the world is too good to waste at a laptop.
The gate opens. The street is there. And
here is the thing that never quite becomes
ordinary, no matter how many times it
happens: the cars are going down the left
side of the road. The trees along the
footpath have purple flowers that are not
like the ones at home. The coffee shop on
the corner sells a flat white, not a drip

coffee with unlimited refills. We are in a different city, in a different part of the world.

That realization — which arrives fresh every time we step through the gate — is not something a schedule produces. It is something the gap produces, over and over, as a gift that does not diminish with repetition.

Three days a week we explore. The city, the suburbs, the coastal path, the neighborhood market that someone mentioned. We head out with a loose idea and no firm plan. We stop when something is interesting. We eat when we are hungry rather than when the reservation says to. We come back when the day has given what it has to give.

One or two days are flex days. The morning is for the project. The afternoon is for wherever the mood takes us — a restaurant area to walk through before dinner, a shopping district to observe, a park to sit in and read. The flex day is the week's permission slip. Nothing is required. Everything is available.

That is the week. Not a system. A texture.

The Work-World Balance

Here is the thing the gap-taker who is also a Maker needs to hear clearly: you will work seven days a week if you let yourself.

Not because the work is oppressive — because the work is yours and it is interesting and there is always more of it and the laptop is always there and the project is always in the back of your mind even when you are walking the coastal path. The Maker who gave fourteen hours a day to someone else's priorities does not suddenly stop being the kind of person who gives fourteen hours. They redirect. The intensity does not disappear. It finds a new object.

This is not a bad quality. It is the quality that makes the Maker's gap productive rather than merely pleasant. But it requires a deliberate counterweight — not a rule about working hours, but a genuine commitment to the other thing the gap is for.

The gap is not only for building something. It is for being somewhere. The two are not in competition, but they require different postures. Building is forward-facing — oriented toward the product, the audience,

339

the outcome. Being is present-facing —
oriented toward the street outside the
gate, the flavor of the coffee, the particular
light of the afternoon in this particular city
that you will not be in forever.

The week that is all building is productive
and slightly hollow. The week that is all
being is rich and slightly formless. The
week that holds both is the week the gap is
designed to produce.

My wife is the external counterweight
when the internal one is not enough. She
knows that sitting at the laptop will not
allow the reset, the refresh, the
reorientation that we came here for. She
knows, and I know, that the work will wait
and the afternoon will not.

The Structure That Is Not a Schedule

The weekly architecture is not a schedule.
Let this be clear before anything else is
said about it.

A schedule is a recreation of the career's
logic applied to the gap's freedom. It is the
person who decides that writing happens
from 8am to 11am, lunch is at noon,
exploration begins at 1pm and ends at

5pm, and the day's events are logged in a journal from 9pm to 9:30. This is not a gap. This is a productivity system wearing a gap's clothes. The schedule defeats the purpose by re-imposing the very rigidity that the career enforced.

What the gap needs instead is the minimum viable structure — the handful of rhythms and choices that give the week enough shape to prevent drift without constraining the specific quality of openness that makes the gap what it is.

The distinction matters because the gap-taker who over-structures is not getting what they paid for. And the gap-taker who under-structures — who lets every day be entirely improvised from the first moment of waking — often finds that the improvisation produces a certain aimlessness that the gap's later stages need to move beyond.

The minimum viable structure looks something like this.

The work has dedicated time

Not scheduled hours with a start and end — dedicated time. The project gets the morning, or the project gets certain days, or the project gets whatever the natural working period is for the person doing it. What matters is that the project does not get crowded out by exploration every day, and that exploration does not get crowded out by the project every day. The week has room for both.

The exploration is intentional without being planned

There is a difference between waking up and deciding to go out and waking up with a specific destination and a timed itinerary. The former is the gap's mode. The latter is tourism. Go somewhere. Have a loose idea about what you want to see or find. Leave room for the thing you did not know was there. Google what is happening in the city this week. Run to catch a train.

The download conversation happens

Even if you have spent every hour of the day together, there is value in the specific kind of conversation that comes from having gone somewhere separately and bringing something back. The separate outing — even a short one, even just a different coffee shop for an hour in the morning — gives each person something to bring to the table that is theirs alone.

One day per week has almost no obligations

The day that does not need to produce anything. No project goals, no exploration itinerary, no family calls to make. The day that exists entirely for whatever presents itself. Sleep until the body is finished sleeping. Read in bed. Walk to wherever the walking leads. This day models what the gap is supposed to feel like even on the weeks when the other days have been busy.

The Week Across the Stages

The weekly architecture looks different depending on which stage of the gap the reader is in. The week that works in Stage One is not the week that works in Stage Three.

Stage One — Decompression. The architecture in Stage One should be minimal. The primary job of Stage One is to let the body and mind decompress. Too much structure in Stage One recreates the career's demand for performance. The week should have mostly open days, some gentle exploration, no project pressure,

343

and whatever amount of sleep the body asks for.

Stage Two — Exploration. The architecture in Stage Two can expand. The curiosity is opening. The world is interesting. The week naturally fills with more exploration, more new places, more of the activity that Stage Two generates spontaneously. The project may begin to appear in Stage Two — tentatively, as an experiment rather than a commitment.

Stage Three — Design. The architecture in Stage Three shifts toward the project. The work is real now, the direction has emerged, the building is underway. The week needs more dedicated work time and more intentional separation between project time and exploration time. Stage Three is when the download conversation becomes most useful, because each person's project has developed enough that there is something substantial to bring back.

Stage Four — Decision. The week in Stage Four holds the work and the reflection simultaneously — the building and the assessing of what the building is becoming. The experiments have produced results. The direction is clarifying. The decision is forming.

The Gate

There is a moment that happens every time we step through the gate and onto the street.

The cars going the wrong way. The purple flowers that are not like the ones at home. The specific quality of light in this particular city. The realization, arriving fresh each time, that we are genuinely somewhere else.

This moment is available every day of the gap. Not just in the first weeks when everything is new and the novelty is overwhelming. Every day, because the place is real and the strangeness is structural and the human capacity to be surprised by a familiar world viewed from a different angle does not diminish with repetition.

The weekly architecture exists to protect this moment. Not to fill every day with productivity — to ensure that most days include the gate, the street, and whatever the afternoon has waiting on the other side of it.

Google what is happening in the city this week. Run to catch a train to somewhere you have not been yet. Stop to watch a boat go by in the harbor.

The boat does not care about your project timeline. The harbor is not impressed by your progress metrics. The afternoon light will not wait for you to finish one more thing before it changes.

Step through the gate.

The week takes care of itself.

THE PREPARATION

Chapters 17 – 19

The pre-gap timeline

CHAPTER SEVENTEEN

The Pre-Gap Timeline: 12 Months Out

I made a list.

It started as fifteen companies I needed to call. Banks, insurance providers, credit card issuers, the auto insurance company, the health insurance company, the pharmacy for the blood pressure prescription. Fifteen calls, I figured. A long Saturday. Done by dinner.

Three days later the list was thirty companies. Then came the apps — six, then eight, then more. A VPN I had not known I needed. A portable monitor for the laptop because I was going to be writing and researching on the road and a single screen was not going to be enough. A virtual mailbox service. A new banking app. An international phone plan. A travel insurance policy that turned out to be the wrong kind, which I only discovered after reading the fine print on page eleven.

I used AI to help me build the initial list. It did a reasonable job. But it missed things — not because it was wrong about what it included but because I had not yet given it a comprehensive picture of my own life. I did not know what I did not know. The list it built was the list of someone who understood the problem. I was still figuring out what the problem was.

It felt like a full-time job for two weeks.

And then, while researching this book, I kept finding things I had missed. Better options. Smarter strategies. Services I had never heard of. Ways to save money I thought I had already wrung out. The preparation I had thought was thorough turned out to be a first draft.

That is why this chapter — and the two that follow it — exist.

Not to make the preparation feel overwhelming. To make it feel manageable. To give you the comprehensive picture I did not have when I started, so that your list begins closer to the finished version rather than growing for three weeks before it stabilizes.

The Golden Gap requires preparation. Real preparation. The kind that takes months, not a long Saturday. But the preparation is also the beginning of the gap itself — the first evidence that you are building something deliberate rather than waiting for permission. Every call you make, every account you notify, every decision you resolve is a small act of commitment. The list is not the obstacle to the Golden Gap. It is the gap, already beginning.

Start here. Twelve months out.

Why Twelve Months Is Not Too Early

Most people underestimate the lead time the pre-gap preparation actually requires.

The Reddit couple who documented their transition most honestly started the process in September 2015 and did not depart until February 2017. Seventeen months. Not because they were slow or indecisive but because the actual work — the home, the possessions, the financial restructuring, the family time, the health preparation — takes longer than expected when you are doing it alongside a full-time job and a full life.

Twelve months is not paranoid. It is realistic. And several items on the twelve-month list have hard deadlines that cannot be compressed regardless of how motivated you are.

Global Entry processing currently takes up to twelve months. Passport renewal through standard channels takes eight to twelve weeks but can take longer at peak periods. The Roth conversion ladder strategy requires five years of lead time for penalty-free access — but the sooner you start the conversions, the sooner the clock starts. Major health work — surgery, dental reconstruction, any elective procedure you have been deferring — needs to be scheduled, completed, and recovered from before departure.

Twelve months is the minimum for a clean, unhurried departure. Eighteen is better. Start now regardless of when you intend to leave.

The Home Decision

The single most consequential pre-gap decision most people face is what to do with the home.

There are four options. Each has real financial and practical implications. None is universally right.

Sell. The cleanest exit. It converts your largest illiquid asset into capital, eliminates property tax, insurance, and maintenance obligations during the gap, and removes the psychological weight of a property requiring management from afar. The disadvantage is irreversibility — if the gap becomes the life, selling was the right call, but if you return and want to re-establish in the same area, you are re-entering a market that has likely moved. Selling makes most sense if you are genuinely uncertain whether you will return, if the equity is meaningful enough to materially improve your gap finances, or if the property has been a source of stress rather than security.

Rent. Generates income that offsets gap costs, preserves the asset, and maintains a home base for eventual return. The disadvantage is the management burden — even with a property manager, you will deal with tenant issues, maintenance decisions, and periodic vacancies from abroad. Some people find this manageable. Others find it the constant background noise that prevents genuine decompression. Renting makes most sense if the rental income is significant relative to gap costs, if you have a trusted local property manager, and if you are genuinely comfortable managing landlord responsibilities while living in Lisbon.

Lock and leave. What we did. The home sits empty, secured, maintained minimally. No rental income. No tenant complications. The property is there when you return, exactly as you left it.

We unplugged everything not related to security cameras or WiFi. We could have switched off the breakers for the hot water heater and stove, but we did not want the house to look completely abandoned to anyone looking through a window. We left some papers on the counter, a few half-empty water bottles, a bowl with a spoon on the kitchen island. If someone looked in, it should appear as though someone had been there that morning and would be back by evening.

It is a small thing. But small things matter when a house is sitting empty for months.

Lock and leave makes most sense if you own your home outright or carry a modest mortgage, if the carrying costs during the gap are manageable within your budget, and if the simplicity of not managing a rental relationship is worth the foregone income.

Downsize before departure. Some people use the pre-gap period to make a move they had been considering — from a large suburban home to a smaller apartment or condo designed for the lock-and-leave life. Lower carrying costs, easier security, and the psychological clarity of having already made the next home decision.

Whichever option you choose, make the decision at twelve months out. The home question, left unresolved, generates anxiety that contaminates everything else in the preparation.

The Stuff Decision

The home decision and the stuff decision are related but distinct.

The home question is about the asset. The stuff question is about everything inside it.

One couple documented their transition honestly: they went from a large home with two cars and accumulated possessions to twelve boxes stored in a family member's garage. No regrets, they reported. But the process took the full seventeen months of their preparation. Stuff takes longer to deal with than money, documents, or technology — not because it is practically complicated but because it is emotionally complicated.

You are not just sorting possessions. You are sorting the physical residue of a life. The things you kept because you might need them someday. The things you kept because they were gifts. The things you kept because getting rid of them felt like admitting something. The things you kept because you simply never decided not to.

The stuff decision has three categories.

Store. A climate-controlled storage unit for furniture, heirlooms, and anything with genuine value that you want when you return. Budget $150 to $300 per month for a decent unit. Do not store things out of indecision — storage costs real money over a twelve-month gap and the things inside it will feel more remote and less important every month you are away.

Give, sell, or donate. Start with the largest items. Furniture that will not survive the gap period. Electronics that will be outdated on your return. Clothing that does not work for slow travel. Books, kitchen equipment, accumulated household items that served the suburban life but have no role in what comes next. Facebook Marketplace, estate sale companies, and donation pickups make this easier than it once was.

Take. You are going to be surprised how little this category contains. The slow traveler lives out of luggage. The stuff that comes with you is what fits in two bags per person — and experienced slow travelers almost universally report that even that is too much initially. You will ship things home within the first month. Plan for this.

Start the stuff decision at twelve months out. Do not leave it for the final weeks. The emotional weight of the stuff decision, compressed into a departure deadline, is one of the most common sources of pre-gap regret.

The Passport and Documents Sprint

Passport renewal. Renew if your passport expires within twelve months of your planned departure date — not six months, twelve. Most of Asia and Africa require six months of passport validity beyond your entry date. Airlines frequently apply the same rule as a blanket policy. Schengen countries require three months of validity beyond your planned departure from the zone. When you renew, request the large book — extra pages at no additional cost. A year of active slow travel will fill a standard passport.

Global Entry. Apply now. Processing currently takes up to twelve months and approval requires an in-person interview at an enrollment center. Global Entry costs $120 for five years and includes TSA PreCheck. For the Golden Gap reader who will be re-entering the United States multiple times during the gap, Global Entry is the difference between forty-five minutes in the immigration hall and eight minutes through the dedicated lane. Several credit cards cover the Global Entry fee as an annual benefit — Chase Sapphire Reserve, American Express Platinum, and Capital One Venture X all currently offer this.

International driving permit. If you plan to rent cars during the gap, get an international driving permit before departure. AAA issues them for $20, requires two passport photos, and the process takes ten minutes in a AAA office. The permit is valid for one year. Without one, you may be legally unable to rent a car in certain countries regardless of your valid US license.

Make copies of everything. Passport bio page, Global Entry card, driver's license, credit cards front and back, health insurance cards, international insurance policy. Store digital copies in a secure cloud folder. Give physical copies to one trusted person at home. Keep a set in your luggage separate from the originals.

The Financial Architecture

The financial preparation for the Golden Gap is not a single task. It is a set of decisions that need to be made in the right order with the right professional guidance.

Consult a fee-only financial advisor who specializes in early retirement. Do this first. Before you make any other financial decisions. Budget $500 to $1,000 for a comprehensive consultation. The XY Planning Network at xyplanningnetwork.com is the right starting point — it was founded by early retirement specialists and has a category filter for advisors with this specific expertise.

The advisor consultation should cover: your actual gap-sized portfolio number based on realistic geographic arbitrage spending, the Roth conversion ladder strategy and whether your current account structure supports it, ACA income management strategy for US-visit years, state residency implications if you plan to be absent for extended periods, and the tax implications of any investment moves you make before departure.

One hour with the right advisor will save you more money than any other item on this list.

The Roth Conversion Ladder. If you have pre-tax retirement savings in a traditional IRA or 401(k), the Roth conversion ladder is worth understanding. Converting traditional IRA funds to Roth IRA in amounts equal to the standard deduction — $29,200 for a couple in 2024 — generates zero federal income tax on the conversion while simultaneously moving money into an account from which withdrawals will be tax-free. Converted funds become accessible without penalty five years after conversion. Start the conversions now.

The ACA Strategy. By managing your taxable income in years when you return to the US for extended visits, you may qualify for substantial ACA subsidies — potentially covering your entire premium for a high-deductible plan. This requires coordination with your financial advisor and advance planning about which years you will carry a US policy. Done correctly, this has produced zero-premium US health insurance for gap travelers with investment portfolios well above the median.

Your gap-sized portfolio number. This is different from your retirement number. The retirement number funds thirty years of life at your current US lifestyle cost. The gap number funds one to three years of slow travel life at geographic arbitrage rates. A couple spending $35,000 per year during the gap needs $35,000 per year in accessible funds. Know your number and know where it is coming from before you book the first flight.

Notify your financial institutions. Every bank, brokerage, and credit card issuer needs to know you are leaving. Not a travel notification — a standing notification that you will be making transactions in multiple countries over an extended period. Some institutions require this in writing. Failure to notify is one of the primary causes of frozen accounts and declined transactions abroad.

Check all card expiry dates. Credit and debit cards expire. A card that expires eight months into your gap will be declined in a city where you have no branch and no way to receive a replacement quickly. Identify every card you plan to use. Note its expiry date. If it expires during your planned gap period, request a replacement now.

The Family Destinations

At twelve months out, your family still has full access to you in the way they have always had access to you. You are geographically proximate. You are available for Sunday lunches and unexpected phone calls and the spontaneous visit that does not require international coordination.

That access is about to change. Not end — the gap does not remove family from your life. But the pattern changes, and the pattern change deserves acknowledgment and deliberate management before departure.

Schedule the family destinations now. Not vague intentions to spend time with people before you leave. Specific dates, booked in the calendar, treated with the same seriousness you would bring to booking a month in Lisbon. A week with your parents. Four days with your adult children. A long weekend with the sibling you have been meaning to see properly for three years.

The pre-gap window is finite and unrepeatable. You are still the version of yourself that shows up at Sunday lunch. After departure the relationships will survive and many will deepen. But the casual, proximate, spontaneous access your family currently has to you is a specific thing that is about to change. Use it while it is still the default.

Have the conversations that tend to get deferred when everyone is busy. With elderly parents especially — are there things that need to be said? Decisions that need to be made? Histories that need to be captured? The pre-gap period is the right time for these conversations, when you are still present and unhurried.

And tell people what you are doing and why. Not to seek permission or manage judgment — to give the people who love you the framework to understand and support a decision that may look, from the outside, like an abrupt departure from the expected script. The people who understand the Golden Gap become your community of support during it.

The Health Sprint

The pre-gap health sprint is not optional. It is the most important preparation on this list for readers over fifty.

Comprehensive medical review. Schedule a full physical with blood work, including a baseline cardiovascular workup, before departure. The gap will likely improve most of your health markers — the biometric data from sabbatical

research is consistent on this. But you
need to know your baseline, have your
conditions documented, and have a plan
for ongoing management before you leave.
If anything significant turns up, deal with it
now.

The dental sprint. Every piece of
deferred dental work gets done before
departure. Every. Single. One. You have
been putting off the crown, the implant,
the deep cleaning, the wisdom tooth that
has been quietly problematic for two years.
Do all of it now, in your own dental office,
with your own dentist who knows your
history, at US insurance rates. Finding a
reliable dentist abroad is one of the most
consistently documented frustrations of
long-term slow travel.

Vision. Update your glasses or contact
lens prescription. Order a backup pair of
glasses. If you wear contacts, calculate
your supply needs for the gap period and
order accordingly.

Elective procedures. If there is anything
you have been considering — a joint that
needs attention, a procedure you have
been scheduling and rescheduling — the

window before the gap is the time. Recover at home. Leave healthy.

This chapter continues in Chapter 18: The Pre-Gap Timeline — Six Months Out

CHAPTER EIGHTEEN

The Pre-Gap Timeline: 6 Months Out

The twelve-month work cleared the big structural decisions. The home is decided. The financial architecture is in motion. The health sprint is underway. The family dates are in the calendar.

Six months out, the work shifts from structural to operational. This is where the list that started at fifteen companies became thirty. Where the apps accumulated. Where the VPN appeared. Where you discover that the infrastructure of your daily life — the banking, the phone, the mail, the insurance, the medications — was more complicated than you thought, and untangling it requires more lead time than you would expect.

Give this phase the same focused attention you gave the twelve-month work. It is less emotionally heavy. It is more technically detailed. And getting it wrong has more immediate consequences — a frozen bank account in Vienna, a declined credit card in Chiang Mai, a prescription you cannot refill in Lisbon — than almost any other category of preparation.

The Insurance Architecture

International health insurance. The correct product for the Golden Gap is not travel insurance. Travel insurance is designed for vacations — it covers trip cancellation, lost luggage, and emergency medical care sufficient to stabilize you for repatriation. It explicitly excludes continuous travel beyond 45 days. Allianz's annual plans, despite using the word "annual," cap individual trip coverage at 45 days. This is the wrong product for a six-month or twelve-month gap.

The correct product is an international health insurance policy designed for long-term nomadic travel. Key features to look for: coverage for a minimum of 12 months continuously, high deductible options ($2,500 to $5,000 per person), coverage ceiling of at least $500,000, emergency evacuation coverage, and the ability to renew while abroad.

The high deductible strategy deserves emphasis. International healthcare outside the United States is dramatically cheaper than American healthcare. A broken wrist in Budapest — five doctor visits, four x-rays, three casts at a top private clinic —

cost $831 total. Cash price. The catastrophic event is what requires insurance: the traffic accident, the appendectomy, the cardiac event. Routine care can be paid out of pocket almost everywhere you are likely to travel. A $5,000 deductible policy covering $500,000 in catastrophic care costs approximately $900 to $1,100 per year for a couple in their fifties.

Carriers worth evaluating: IMG Global and Cigna Global are the two most consistently recommended by long-term travelers with actual claims experience. Avoid World Nomads for extended travel — the coverage is limited relative to cost and the recommendations are largely affiliate-driven. SafetyWing prices less favorably for the 50+ reader.

Read the policy documents. All of them. Insurance companies do not make money by paying claims. Know what is and is not covered, how the claims process works, and what documentation is required before you need to use it.

The ACA US health insurance strategy. If you plan to return to the United States for extended visits during the gap, you may need US health insurance for those periods. By managing your taxable income — keeping it low in years when you plan to be in the US — you may qualify for substantial subsidies, potentially covering your premium entirely. Coordinate your US visit timing and income recognition with your financial advisor. Do not carry an ACA policy in years when you will spend minimal time in the US — the policy offers zero coverage abroad.

Auto insurance. Here is the honest answer that most planning guides skip entirely.

The fabled "garaged car" insurance plan — the dramatically reduced policy for a vehicle in storage that is not being driven — is largely a myth in most states. What actually happens depends entirely on your state's minimum coverage requirements.

In most states, you cannot drop below the state minimum liability coverage without ending the vehicle's registration. And ending the registration creates complications when you want to re-register upon return. The practical solution: drop your coverage to the absolute state minimum allowed while maintaining valid registration. Call your insurer, explain that the vehicle will be garaged and unused for an extended period, ask specifically what the minimum coverage option is while maintaining registration, and make that change. The savings vary by state but are real. Do some research on your specific state — some states may have more options than others.

If you have two vehicles and will not be using either during the gap, consider whether to sell one. The insurance, registration, and depreciation costs of an unused second vehicle over a twelve-month gap add up to real money.

Homeowner's or renter's insurance. If you are locking and leaving your home, notify your homeowner's insurance company. Some policies have vacancy clauses that void or reduce coverage after a property has been unoccupied for thirty to sixty days. Know what your policy says before you leave, not after something happens.

The Banking Stack

The non-negotiable: Charles Schwab checking account. Schwab's checking account reimburses all ATM fees worldwide at the end of each month, with no foreign transaction fees. This is the single most important banking product for the slow traveler. Every other bank charges fees for international ATM withdrawals and foreign currency transactions. Schwab reimburses them all. If you do not have a Schwab checking account, open one now — the account requires a small initial deposit and a few weeks to set up properly.

Wise. The Wise account and debit card converts currency at the mid-market rate with minimal fees and operates in 174 countries. Use it for local currency withdrawals and purchases in countries where you want to minimize exchange rate losses. The Wise app shows you the exact rate you are getting in real time.

Revolut. Useful for currency management and international transfers. Some travelers use Revolut as their primary travel card. The free tier is sufficient for most gap needs.

Credit cards for travel. The best travel credit cards earn points on everyday spending and offer meaningful travel benefits. Chase Sapphire Preferred or Reserve, American Express Gold or Platinum, and Capital One Venture X are the most consistently valuable for slow travelers. Key features to confirm before departure: no foreign transaction fees, travel insurance benefits, and the Global Entry fee credit if you have not already used it.

Notify every institution. Every bank, credit union, brokerage, and credit card issuer needs a standing note in your account that you will be making transactions internationally for an extended period. Call each one. Ask specifically what they recommend for customers traveling long-term. Some require written notification.

Emergency cash. Carry the equivalent of $300 to $500 in US dollars as emergency backup. Not for day-to-day use — for the moment when every card is declined, the ATM is broken, and you need to get somewhere. Cash solves problems that technology cannot. Keep it separate from your wallet.

The Phone and Connectivity Stack

Keep your US number active. Your US phone number is attached to more of your life than you realize. Bank two-factor authentication. Government accounts. Subscription services. Healthcare providers. The number that your family and friends have had for years. Do not cancel it. The cheapest way to maintain it: Google Fi has an affordable low-use option, or port your number to a Voice over IP service. The goal is a number that can receive calls and texts, including verification codes, for $10 to $20 per month.

Two-factor authentication migration — do this before you leave. This is the item that most people miss and most regret. If your bank, email, or any important account sends verification codes to your US phone number, you are vulnerable the moment your US phone stops working reliably abroad. Before departure, switch every important account from SMS-based two-factor authentication to an authenticator app — Google Authenticator or Authy are the standard options. This takes an afternoon. Do it before you need it.

eSIM for international data. Modern smartphones support eSIM — a digital SIM activated remotely without a physical card. They also might have a physical SIM. You can use both at the same time. For each country or region you travel in, purchase a local or regional data eSIM. Keep your home physical SIM in the phone. Airalo, Holafly, and Saily are the main providers. Costs run $16 to $20 for 5GB of regional data. eSIMDB.com allows price comparison across providers.

Google Voice. Set up a Google Voice number before you leave the United States, if needed. Google Voice requires a US IP address to activate — you cannot set it up from abroad. Once active, it provides a US phone number that can make and receive calls and texts over WiFi from anywhere in the world.

WhatsApp. Set it up before departure. WhatsApp is the universal communication platform in Europe, Latin America, Southeast Asia, and most of the world outside North America. Locals, landlords, tour guides, markets, restaurants — all of them communicate via WhatsApp. Without it, you are operating with a significant communication handicap.

VPN. A VPN serves three functions during the gap. It secures your connection on public WiFi networks, protecting your banking and personal data. It prevents some banks from freezing accounts when they detect a foreign IP address. And it allows you to access home-country streaming services that are geographically restricted. NordVPN at approximately $4 per month and Surfshark at approximately $2.50 per month are the two most recommended options. Proton VPN has a functional free tier.

Virtual mailbox. Your US mail does not stop because you leave. Bills, financial statements, jury summons, tax documents, medical correspondence — it will continue to arrive at your US address. A virtual mailbox service scans your mail and delivers it digitally. Anytime Mailbox operates in more than forty countries and costs $5 to $10 per month. Set it up sixty days before departure minimum. One honest warning: pricing is set by operators and some have received complaints about unexpected billing increases. Use a credit card with good dispute resolution as your payment method.

Portable monitor. If you plan to work, write, research, or manage finances during the gap, a second screen makes the difference between sustainable and frustrating. A quality portable USB-C monitor weighs under two pounds and costs $150 to $250. This was one of the items on my list I did not anticipate needing until I thought through what a working day on the road would actually look like. I have not regretted it.

The Medication Strategy

The 90-day supply. Most US health insurance plans allow only a 30-day supply per prescription fill. For a gap of six months or more, you need to solve this before departure. The solution is the vacation override — a provision most insurers offer that allows a 90-day supply when travel is documented. Call your insurer and your pharmacy. Ask specifically about the vacation override process. Some require a letter from your physician. Start this conversation four to six weeks before departure.

Controlled substances. This requires special attention. Medications that are legal in the United States with a prescription may be illegal, restricted, or require special documentation in other countries — including countries you transit through on layovers.

ADHD medications including Adderall are illegal in Japan regardless of US prescription. Benzodiazepines including Xanax are restricted or require special permits in the UAE, many Southeast Asian countries, and others. Sleep aids, opioid-based pain medications, and some anxiety medications fall into similar categories in various jurisdictions.

Check every country on your itinerary — including layover countries — against the International Narcotics Control Board traveler information at incb.org/travellers. If you carry a controlled substance into a restricted country, the consequences can be severe regardless of your US prescription.

For travel through Schengen countries with controlled substances, a Schengen Certificate from your physician is the standard documentation. This is a specific form available from your doctor that certifies your prescription and the medical necessity of the medication.

Medical documentation packet. Before departure, compile a single document containing: your blood type, all current medications with both brand and generic names, all known allergies with reaction descriptions, all current medical conditions, your primary care physician's name and contact information, your international insurance policy number and emergency contact, and emergency contacts for family. Keep a digital copy in secure cloud storage and a physical copy in your luggage separate from your passport.

The generic name requirement is important. Brand names vary by country. A physician in Budapest or Chiang Mai needs to know the generic compound, not the US brand name.

The WiFi Research Protocol

Not all destinations have equal WiFi quality. For the Golden Gap reader who plans to write, work, manage finances, or stay in regular contact with family, WiFi quality is a real selection criterion — not an afterthought.

Before committing to a base camp city, research: the average broadband speeds in that city, the typical WiFi quality in monthly rental apartments, whether the city has coworking spaces as a backup option, and whether the mobile data coverage is reliable enough to use a hotspot when apartment WiFi fails.

Chiang Mai, Medellín, Lisbon, Tbilisi, and most major European cities have excellent connectivity by any standard. Some otherwise attractive destinations — certain beach towns, rural areas, parts of Southeast Asia outside major cities — have connectivity that makes sustained work difficult.

Check Numbeo.com for average internet speeds by city. Read recent reviews of apartments in your target base camp with specific attention to WiFi comments. And always ask the host directly — "what is the upload and download speed?" — before booking for a month.

This chapter continues in Chapter 19: The Pre-Gap Timeline — Final 90 Days

CHAPTER NINETEEN

The Pre-Gap Timeline: Final 90 Days

The structural decisions are made. The operational infrastructure is built. The banking stack is configured, the insurance is in place, the medications are sorted, the virtual mailbox is redirecting your mail.

The final ninety days are the last mile. The work shifts from building to testing, from planning to confirming, from deciding to executing.

This phase has a different emotional texture than the twelve-month and six-month phases. The earlier work felt like preparation for something that was still abstract. The final ninety days are different. The departure date is on the calendar. The reservation is booked. The gap is no longer a plan. It is a schedule.

Some people find this phase exhilarating. Some find it terrifying. Most find it both, simultaneously, on alternating days. All of this is normal. The chapter closes with what the first week will actually feel like — because knowing it in advance makes it significantly more manageable.

90 Days Out — Accommodation and Transport

Book the first base camp. This is the moment to commit. The apartment for the first month or six weeks of the gap should be booked now if you have not already. This is not the time for maximum flexibility — the best apartments in the best locations book out months in advance. Search Airbnb with monthly dates. Look for properties with a minimum of fifty reviews and a 4.8 rating or above. Read the most recent reviews specifically. Ask the host directly about WiFi speeds before booking.

The first base camp deserves more attention than subsequent ones because it is where Phase 1 — Decompression — happens. It should be comfortable, well-equipped with a proper kitchen, in a walkable neighborhood, and in a city that is genuinely interesting without being overwhelming. Lisbon, Chiang Mai, Medellín, and Porto are among the most consistently recommended first base camps for exactly these reasons.

Do not try to plan the entire gap at booking. Know the first two stops. Have a rough sketch of the third. Leave the rest open.

Book inbound transport. Flights booked 90 days in advance typically offer better pricing than last-minute purchases for international routes. Use Google Flights to track prices and set alerts. Book directly with the airline when possible — it simplifies changes, cancellations, and assistance if something goes wrong.

If you are starting with a repositioning cruise as your Phase 1 decompression — the floating hotel that handles all logistics while your nervous system recalibrates — book now. Repositioning cruises run $60 to $100 per person per day all-inclusive and typically operate in shoulder season when demand is lower.

60 Days Out — The Home and the Stuff

Execute the home preparation. Whatever your home decision — sell, rent, lock-and-leave — the execution happens now. If selling, the property should be on the market or under contract. If renting, the tenant should be identified and the lease signed. If locking and leaving, work through this checklist:

- Notify your homeowner's insurance company of the extended vacancy

- Install or verify security cameras with remote monitoring

- Set interior lights on timers — not the same pattern every day

- Ask a trusted neighbor to collect any packages or mail that arrives before the virtual mailbox redirect is complete

- Stop all delivery subscriptions — meal kits, newspapers, anything on auto-delivery to your physical address

- Forward your mail or redirect it to your virtual mailbox

- Unplug all non-essential electronics

- Turn the water heater to vacation mode if your unit has it

- Leave the property looking inhabited — papers on a counter, something in the kitchen that suggests recent presence

- Give a spare key to one trusted person locally

Complete the stuff decision. The donation run, the storage unit, the final sale of anything remaining. This is the deadline. What is not dealt with by sixty days out will either go into storage at cost or will be abandoned in a rush.

Cancel or redirect recurring services. Streaming subscriptions tied to your US address. Gym memberships. Local delivery services. Any subscription you are paying for a physical location or US-only service you will not be using. Make a list of every recurring charge on every credit card. Evaluate each one. Cancel what you will not use. Some subscriptions — Spotify, Netflix, cloud storage — remain useful internationally and are worth keeping.

30 Days Out — Technology and Testing

Test every system. Do not assume your digital infrastructure works because you set it up. Test it. Log into your bank accounts using your VPN. Confirm the VPN does not trigger fraud alerts or lockouts. Make a small international transfer through Wise to verify the account is active. Load your eSIM provider app and confirm your account is ready to purchase a plan. Log into your virtual mailbox and verify it is receiving redirected mail.

Activate your authenticator app. Go through every important account — banking, email, investment accounts, Social Security, Medicare, healthcare providers — and verify that two-factor authentication is routed through your authenticator app rather than your US phone number. This task takes several hours if done properly. Do it now rather than at the airport.

Download offline maps. Google Maps allows you to download city and regional maps for offline use. Download the maps for your first base camp city and surrounding region before departure. Data may be limited or unavailable during transit. An offline map is the difference between confident navigation and standing on a street corner with a dead phone.

Configure your devices for international use. Confirm your phone is carrier-unlocked — you will need this to use international eSIMs. If it is locked, contact your carrier now. Unlocking can take several days and requires the account to be in good standing.

The portable monitor test. If you purchased one, test it with your laptop at home. Confirm the cable compatibility, the display settings, and the charging setup. Discover and solve any technical issues now rather than in your first base camp apartment.

2 Weeks Out — The Final Administration

Healthcare loose ends. Confirm your travel medicine appointment is complete and all recommended vaccines are administered with sufficient time for immunity to develop. Confirm your 90-day medication supply is in hand. Confirm your medical documentation packet is compiled and stored in both digital and physical formats.

Financial final check. Confirm all institution notifications are on file. Check the expiry dates of all cards you are carrying one final time. Confirm your emergency cash is ready. Download your bank and investment apps and verify they work correctly. Set up account alerts for unusual transactions on all cards — this is your early warning system for compromised cards while abroad.

The subscription audit — final pass. Go through your bank and credit card statements one more time looking for recurring charges you missed the first time. They are always there.

Family final visits. If you scheduled family destination visits as recommended at twelve months out, most of these should be complete. Use the final two weeks for the quieter, less formal connection — the dinner rather than the trip, the phone call rather than the event. The people who matter know you are going. They know you will be in contact. The relationship does not require a farewell ceremony. It requires presence, which you can still provide until the morning you leave.

The Day Before

Pack your bags the day before. Not the morning of.

Packing the morning of a major departure introduces a category of stress that is completely avoidable. Pack the day before. Sleep. Leave with a clear head.

Two bags per person is the working standard for long-term slow travel. One checked bag, one carry-on. Experienced slow travelers eventually get this down to carry-on only. For the first gap, two bags is fine — you will ship things home within the first month regardless.

What to bring: clothing for the climate you are entering plus one layer warmer than you expect to need. All medications in carry-on luggage — never checked. All electronics and cables in carry-on. Physical documents including passport, Global Entry card, international insurance card, and medical documentation packet in a dedicated folder that goes in the bag you carry on your person.

What not to bring: more than you can carry comfortably for thirty minutes through an airport. You will regret every extra pound by day three.

What the First Week Actually Feels Like

Nobody tells you this part. So I will.

The first week of the Golden Gap does not feel like freedom. It feels strange.

The structure that organized your life for thirty years is gone. The inbox is not filling. The phone is not demanding. The calendar is empty in a way it has not been since you were a teenager. You have done what you planned to do. You are where you planned to be. And instead of the liberation you expected, you feel — on alternating hours — a low-level disorientation that you cannot quite name.

This is the Decompression phase beginning. It is normal. It is documented by every long-term traveler who has been honest about their first weeks. The nervous system is recalibrating. The body is releasing stress markers that have been present so long they feel like the baseline. The identity that was built around professional contribution is standing in a beautiful apartment in a foreign city with nowhere to be and nothing required of it.

It does not know what to do yet. That is fine. It will figure it out.

The disorientation typically peaks around day three and begins to lift around day seven. The second week is better than the first. The third week is when the place starts to feel like somewhere you live rather than somewhere you are visiting. The fourth week is where the Golden Gap actually begins — where the design work starts, where the curiosity box opens, where the question of who you are without the title starts getting interesting answers.

Give yourself the first week. Do not judge the gap by the first week. Do not judge yourself by how you feel in the first week. The instrument is recalibrating. The data from the first week is noise.

By week four you will wonder why you waited so long.

Five Honest Reflections

> *One: The preparation is not the obstacle to the Golden Gap. It is the gap beginning. Every call you make, every account you notify, every decision you resolve is a small act of commitment to the life you are building.*
>
> *Two: The list will grow. That is not a sign that something is wrong. It is a sign that you are developing a comprehensive picture of your own life — something most people have never been forced to do. The growing list is the work.*
>
> *Three: The home question and the stuff question are the two most emotionally demanding items on the timeline. Give them the most lead time and the most honest attention. The decisions you defer here become the decisions you regret.*
>
> *Four: Test everything before you need it. The technology that fails in Vienna is the technology you assumed was working*

because you set it up six months ago. The 30-day test run is not optional.

Five: The first week will not feel like what you expected. The gap you planned for starts in week four. Give yourself the grace of the transition.

WHAT COMES AFTER

Chapter 20

The life the gap builds

The Gap Doesn't End

We are still in it.

That is the honest answer to the question this chapter is supposed to answer. I am writing this from inside the gap, not from the other side of it. The flight back to Dallas exists on a calendar somewhere but the date is soft. We are already talking about whether to extend — another city in this part of the world, another few weeks, another gate to step through onto another street with the cars going the wrong way and the flowers being different. Whether that happens depends on variables we cannot yet resolve. The income traction. My father's health. Our need, which is real and not shameful, to sleep in our own bed.

Nothing is set in stone.

That uncertainty used to feel like a problem. Now it feels like the point.

The gap did not give me a five-year plan. It gave me something more useful: the ability to be in an uncertain situation without needing it to resolve immediately. The patience to let the variables work themselves out. The specific confidence that comes from having already made the hard decision and survived it and found the water was not cold.

What comes after the gap is different for every person who takes one. But here is what I know from where I am standing: the gap does not end when you book the flight home. It does not end when you unpack the bags and reconnect the printer and start answering emails again. The gap ends — if it ends at all — when the operating system reverts. When the anxiety comes back as the primary fuel. When the inbox becomes the first thing and the last thing and the thing that buzzes in your pocket during dinner.

That reversion is not inevitable. The gap changes something that does not have to change back.

—

The Three Paths — In Full

Stage Four arrives differently for every gap-taker. For some it is a clear decision made on a specific afternoon. For most it is a gradual recognition — a direction that has been forming for months finally becoming legible enough to act on.

Three paths forward. Not a menu — a set of possibilities that the gap itself helps sort.

The Return

The Return is not failure. This point deserves emphasis because the culture around extended breaks tends to romanticize the radical departure and treat going back as a retreat from the vision.

Most people who take the gap and return to something resembling traditional employment do not return to what they left. They return to a version of professional engagement that the gap redesigned — different terms, different balance, different clarity about what the work needs to feel like and what it is not allowed to cost.

The person who returns knows things they did not know before. They know which parts of the career identity were genuinely theirs. They know how much the Convenience Premium was costing them and they will not pay all of it again. They know what the mornings feel like when the inbox does not own them. They know what their partner looks like when the stress drain is not running. They know what they are capable of building when the time belongs to them.

They take all of that back into the professional world. And the professional world, experienced from that vantage point, is a different place.

The Return is not retreat. It is re-engagement on new terms — by someone who has done the research that most people never do.

The Reinvent

The Reinvent is the path the book's narrative has been building toward — the Maker who has been making, the direction that emerged from Stage Two and was tested in Stage Three, the income that is developing toward something real.

The Reinvent requires patience that most people underestimate before taking the gap and overestimate once they are in it. The consulting practice that was supposed to have its first client in month two has it in month seven. The book that was supposed to find its audience in the first year is still building that audience in year two. The content creation that produces modest income in month six produces meaningful income in month eighteen.

The Reinvent rewards staying with it past the point where the external skeptics were sure it had not worked. The internal skeptic quiets as the evidence accumulates. The income follows the work, not the other way around.

Going back into the corporate world is the last resort — not because corporate work is shameful but because the direction has been identified and the work toward it is underway and abandoning that work at the first sign of difficulty is the decision that is hardest to recover from. The gap revealed the direction. The Reinvent honors it.

Maybe there is a job in a different country, where the work-life balance is genuinely different and the skills developed over a career have genuine value in a market that has not been saturated by them. Maybe that is not the corporate re-entry — maybe that is a different version of the Reinvent, in a different place, on different terms. Nothing is set in stone. That is the Reinvent's specific quality: it remains open to the direction the evidence suggests rather than the direction the plan assumed.

The Extend

The Extend is the path that surprises the most people who end up taking it — because most of them did not intend to.

They planned a six-month gap. At month four they realized the direction needed more time. At month six the income was beginning to develop but not yet at the level that made returning feel necessary. At month eight they were somewhere they had not planned to be and it was working in ways they had not anticipated. The decision to extend was not a decision to abandon the original plan. It was the recognition that the original plan was more conservative than the situation required.

The Extend is available to anyone whose financial architecture can support it — and for many gap-takers, the geographic arbitrage that the gap provides makes the extension significantly more affordable than they feared. The month in Chiang Mai that costs $1,400 for two people is not a month of burning savings. It is a month of living on approximately what the portfolio generates at a 3.5% withdrawal rate.

The Extend is also available in forms that do not look like continuous international travel. Going home is not ending the gap if the posture toward life does not revert. The person who returns to the United States but keeps the gap's operating system — the curiosity as primary fuel, the project as the organizing purpose, the relationship as the deliberate investment, the Convenience Premium as the thing they will not pay back in full — is still on their gap. Just not in a country outside the US.

It is still a gap. Yes.

The Gap as Operating System

The gap is not a period of time. It is a way of being in time.

The career was also an operating system — one organized around external demands, performance metrics, organizational hierarchy, and the specific anxiety of continuous evaluation. That operating system ran for thirty-five years. It shaped how mornings felt, how decisions were made, what constituted a good day and what constituted a wasted one.

The gap installs a different operating system. One organized around internal direction, self-designed structure, genuine curiosity, and the specific confidence of someone who is building something for themselves rather than performing for someone else's assessment.

The question of whether the gap ends is really the question of whether the operating system reverts.

It does not have to.

The person who returns to traditional employment after the gap does not have to return to the career operating system. They can bring the gap's operating system back into a professional context — the clarity about what the work costs and what it is worth, the deliberate protection of the relationship's resource of presence, the project that exists outside the job and belongs to them regardless of what the job does.

The person who extends the gap internationally does not have to abandon the gap's operating system when the international travel ends. The posture travels. It does not require a specific passport stamp to function.

The person who reinvents does not have to keep the operating system only until the new thing starts generating income. The income is not the operating system. The income is what the operating system produces when it is running well.

The gap ends when you let it end. Not before.

To the Reader Still on the Fence

If you have read this far and you are still sitting on the fence, something needs to be said directly.

If you are thinking about this gap — seriously thinking about it, which is what reading a book about it means — that is not curiosity. That is a signal. The person who is genuinely happy at work, genuinely not exhausted, genuinely not lying in bed on Sunday night with the specific dread of Monday morning, does not buy this book. They do not read this far into it. They do not recognize themselves in every chapter.

You bought this book for a reason.

How many mornings has the alarm gone off and you wished your life was different? How many Sundays has the week ahead felt like something to survive rather than something to inhabit? How many times have you looked at someone who has done something like this and thought 'must be nice' — and then returned to the inbox?

Tomorrow morning could be different.

Not because the gap is easy or risk-free or guaranteed to work out the way the plan assumes. None of those things are true. But because the alarm that does not go off tomorrow morning is the first morning of a different life. The emails that stop arriving are the first evidence that the thing that was consuming your presence has lost its claim on it. The planning that starts — for the flight, for the base camp, for the financial architecture, for the conversation with your parents before you leave — is the work that is finally worth the hours it costs.

That is something to work hard on. For you.

Not for the quarterly numbers. Not for the performance review. Not for the organization that will replace you within a quarter of your departure and remember you warmly at the retirement party and move on.

For you.

The gap does not require perfection of circumstances. It requires enough — enough savings, enough courage, enough honesty about what the current life is actually costing. You have been calculating the cost of the gap for months or years. The calculation you have not done is the cost of not taking it.

The Northern Lights are up there right now. The stairs to the Sydney Opera House still have that particular quality of morning light. The gate is there. The street beyond it is there. The cars are going the wrong way and the flowers are different and the flat white is waiting at the coffee shop on the corner.

The only thing standing between you and that morning is the decision.

What the Life on the Other Side Looks Like

From where I am standing right now —
inside the gap, with the flight home on a
soft date and the extension under
discussion and the income building toward
something but not yet there — the life on
the other side of the decision looks like
this.

It looks uncertain. Not in the way that
uncertainty felt before the gap — the
anxiety-flavored uncertainty of not
knowing if the career would continue, if
the performance would be adequate, if the
organization would survive the next
restructuring. Different uncertainty. The
curiosity-flavored kind. The kind where the
variable that has not resolved is interesting
rather than threatening.

It looks like a decision being made in real
time — not from a spreadsheet but from
the accumulated evidence of the months
that have passed. The experiments that
have run. The results that have come in.
The direction that has clarified even as
specific plans have changed.

It looks like my wife and I talking about
where to go next in the way that people
talk about what to have for dinner — not as
a life-altering deliberation but as a genuine

and interesting question that deserves a genuine and interesting answer.

It looks like the work. The books written. The methodology developing. The audience being built. The income not yet where it needs to be and the absolute certainty that it is coming.

It looks like a life organized around the right priorities in the right order.

That is not a guarantee. It is not a blueprint. It is the view from inside a decision that was hard to make and has not been regretted for a single morning since.

The gap doesn't end.

It becomes what comes after.

And what comes after is still the gap — lived in a different place, at a different pace, with a different set of open questions. But organized around the same thing.

You.

Not the organization. Not the inbox. Not the alarm.

You.

The gap was always for you. It still is.

A Letter to the Reader

From the kitchen counter of a friend's home in Sydney, Australia.

My wife left forty-five minutes ago for a walk down to the harbor. By now she is crossing the Sydney Harbour Bridge on foot — the actual bridge, the one in all the photographs, the one that looked like a postcard until we were living close enough to walk across it on a Tuesday morning because we had nowhere to be. She will stop at her favorite bakery for a spinach roll. She will take the bus back after lunch. She has done this before. She will do it again.

I am sitting here with an Aussie coffee — which is just espresso, but don't tell the Aussies that — listening to the birds outside the open sliding glass door.

I should tell you about the birds.

Australian birds are loud in a way that American birds are not. Not louder exactly — more prehistoric. I told my wife they sound like dinosaurs living in the trees. She laughed and said she does not notice them as much as I do. That is probably because she grew up with them. I did not. I notice them every morning.

That noticing — the specific, uncomplicated pleasure of hearing something for the first time — is what I am writing to tell you about.

—

You just finished a book. That is the first thing to acknowledge.

Not just any book — a book about a life you have not taken yet, or are in the middle of taking, or are sitting on the fence about. You read about the numbers and the stages and the base camps and the skeptics and the experiments. You read about the cliff and the water and the gate and the purple flowers. You read about a couple on a kitchen counter in Australia listening to dinosaur birds while the laundry needs hanging.

Something in you responded to this. Something said yes — or at least maybe — or at least not yet, but I am listening.

That response is not nothing. That response is the beginning.

You have just taken the first step. You have started your list. You now have an educated choice in front of you — not a vague aspiration, not a fantasy, but a real choice with real numbers and a real framework and real people who have done it and documented what it costs and what it gives back.

The choice is this: will you let your body and mind keep telling you that you need this — and do something about it — or will you close this book and return to the thing you were doing before?

—

Here is the one thing I could not fit in any chapter.

You cannot fight nature.

There will come a day — not a dramatic day, not a day that announces itself — when the window closes. When the body renegotiates its terms quietly and the stairs are a different proposition and the twenty-kilometer coastal walk requires more planning than spontaneity. That day is coming for both of us. Not today. Maybe not for years. But it is coming.

You know this. You have watched it happen to people you love. You understand, in the way that only someone who has lived enough of life understands, that the version of you who can do this fully is not permanent.

I am not telling you this to frighten you. I am telling you because you are way past ready for retirement. What you want is your life back. Now. While the noticing is still sharp. While the birds still sound like dinosaurs.

—

Here is the permission.

You have already done harder things than this.

You built a career. You navigated organizations that did not always deserve your effort. You jumped financial hurdles — and yes, you banged a knee on the way over some of them. You may have raised children. You have survived things that were not in the plan and come out the other side of them with the specific, unbreakable self-knowledge of someone who has been genuinely tested.

You can do this.

Not perfectly. Not without the occasional wrong turn or stalled experiment or week when the internal skeptic is louder than usual. I am not doing it perfectly either. I might fail at parts of it. I might not make the money I planned on the timeline I planned. But I have found a kind of wealth in this life that the balance sheet cannot measure.

I am Reclaiming, Resetting, and Repositioning my life after fifty.

I am doing it right now — on a kitchen counter in Sydney, with espresso going cold and laundry waiting and dinosaur birds outside the door and my wife somewhere on the harbour bridge with a spinach roll in her future.

You can do it too.

A Golden Gap is not just for other people. You just needed it defined and your questions answered. I gave you both.

Now go.

MJ Carver

Sydney, Australia

A Note on Research

The Golden Gap is built on two foundations: documented real-world experience and verified data. This book would not exist without the people who blazed the path first — who chose the gap before it had a name, tracked every expense, published every number, and showed the rest of us that the math actually works.

The primary financial anchor throughout this book is the documented experience of Eric and Katie at bonusnachos.com — five years, four continents, nineteen countries, with full financial transparency. Their $28,050 annual average and the category-by-category breakdown in Chapter Seven are their real numbers, publicly shared. The intellectual honesty of their documentation is the standard this book tries to honor.

The research synthesis in this book uses a methodology developed during the gap itself: reading real accounts from gap-takers, slow travelers, and researchers, then using AI-assisted research tools to verify, challenge, or deepen what those accounts reveal. When someone reports that their resting heart rate dropped ten

beats per minute when the sabbatical
began, the methodology asks: does the
data support this? When the experience of
decompression is described, the research
asks: what does the neuroscience actually
show?

That combination — human experience
plus verified evidence — is the book's
epistemology. Neither alone is sufficient.
The anecdote without the data is a story.
The data without the human experience is
a spreadsheet. Together they are a map.

Statistical sources include the Federal
Reserve Survey of Consumer Finances, the
Bureau of Labor Statistics, Numbeo cost-
of-living data, the Global Peace Index, the
Sabbatical Project research led by DJ
DiDonna and Matt Bloom at the University
of Notre Dame, and peer-reviewed
research on burnout, cognitive recovery,
and relationship quality cited throughout
the text.

For those about to widen the path with
their own footsteps: document what you
find. The people who read the next book
about this life will need your numbers too.

About the Author

MJ Carver spent more than three decades in enterprise-level operations and sales leadership, walking ten to twenty miles a day in hundred-degree heat while the metrics of his performance were reviewed in real time from air-conditioned offices hundreds of miles away. He was good at it. He was also, without quite naming it, exhausted by it.

When his position was eliminated, he did not return to the traditional model. He and his Australian wife chose the Golden Gap — a deliberately designed period of reset, exploration, and reinvention that took them to Australia, and from there to the world. He is writing this book from a kitchen counter in Sydney, with espresso going cold and dinosaur birds outside the open sliding glass door.

The Golden Gap is Book Three of The Life Strategy Series. Book One, The Leverage Code, covers building professional position before you need it. Book Two, Spat-Out, covers surviving the involuntary exit when it comes. Book Three is about what you build next.

MJ Carver writes, consults, and continues to develop the AI-plus-human-experience research methodology that produced this book. He believes that the most useful thing any fifty-plus person can do with their accumulated expertise is point it at something that is genuinely theirs.

He is still in the gap. The experiments continue.

Learn more about what MJ is working on at:

www.mjcarverbooks.com

You will find additional 2nd income tips, an AI+Human content machine, and even a way of working with MJ if you need some help.

Also by MJ Carver

The Leverage Code — Book One

Build position before you need it. The strategies, mindset, and practical tools for establishing professional leverage — the kind that survives restructurings, outlasts recessions, and gives you options when options matter most.

Spat-Out — Book Two

Survive the hit when it comes. The honest, practical guide to navigating involuntary career exit — what to do in the first seventy-two hours, how to protect your finances, your identity, and your momentum, and how to design what comes next from the wreckage of what was.

www.ingramcontent.com/pod-product-compliance
Lightning Source LLC
Chambersburg PA
CBHW071445140726

47997CB00005B/1591